Timbrook Library

NO BULL INFORMATION

NO BULL
INFORMATION

*A Humorous, Practical Guide
to Help Americans Adapt
to the Information Age*

Dr. John Gamble

New York

NO BULL INFORMATION
A Humorous, Practical Guide to Help Americans Adapt to the Information Age

© 2015 Dr. John Gamble.

Published in New York, New York, by Morgan James Publishing. Morgan James and The Entrepreneurial Publisher are trademarks of Morgan James, LLC.
www.MorganJamesPublishing.com

The Morgan James Speakers Group can bring authors to your live event. For more information or to book an event visit The Morgan James Speakers Group at www.TheMorganJamesSpeakersGroup.com.

A free eBook edition is available with the purchase of this print book.

CLEARLY PRINT YOUR NAME ABOVE IN UPPER CASE

Instructions to claim your free eBook edition:
1. Download the BitLit app for Android or iOS
2. Write your name in **UPPER CASE** on the line
3. Use the BitLit app to submit a photo
4. Download your eBook to any device

ISBN 978-1-63047-176-7 paperback
ISBN 978-1-63047-179-8 Colored PB
ISBN 978-1-63047-177-4 eBook
ISBN 978-1-63047-178-1 hardcover
Library of Congress Control Number:
2014935530

Cover Design by:
Rachel Lopez
www.r2cdesign.com

Interior Design by:
Bonnie Bushman
bonnie@caboodlegraphics.com

In an effort to support local communities, raise awareness and funds, Morgan James Publishing donates a percentage of all book sales for the life of each book to Habitat for Humanity Peninsula and Greater Williamsburg.

Get involved today, visit
www.MorganJamesBuilds.com

Habitat for Humanity
Peninsula and
Greater Williamsburg
Building Partner

Dedicated to Mary B. Gamble,
1918-2011

love, limericks, laughter

TABLE OF CONTENTS

ARNB SM

Wise advice from a character named Arnbi,
whom you'll meet soon enough:

*Too bad, but "simple" is a square peg that seldom
fits into the round hole that is our modern world.*

A Word about Abbreviations (Acronyms) and Graphics Used in this Book

These are vital to this book. They provide a way to quickly focus on important principles and to show others what we are doing. Take a few minutes to familiarize yourself with these terms.

- First, NBI stands for "No-Bull Information," the theme of this book.
- It is pronounced by saying each letter: N*B*I.
- Arnbi is a character that will be your guide throughout the book. The "Ar" comes from Aristotle, one of the first Western philosophers to carefully examine information. The "Ar" is added in front of NBI, producing Arnbi. Arnbi is pronounced Arn (like in Arnold) and Bee. Say it a couple times, and soon it will sound natural.
- ARNBism is a wise, profound statement made by Arnbi. It is formed by combining "Arnbi" and "ism." Say this out loud: "optimism, ARNBism, optimism, ARNBism."

Read the following a couple times before moving on to the heart of the book. NBI uses Arnbi and the wise, funny things Arnbi says

(ARNBisms) to help us better understand and handle information in the 21st century. It's OK to sing or chant the sentence if this helps.

Below are a few examples of this approach. I hope these will make you smile. But also understand that Arnbi serves a very important, serious function: symbolizing and focusing attention on the most important points of NBI.

 Arnbi standing alone, saddened by the information he confronts.

Arnbi holding a shovel useful for eliminating bull-laden information.

 ARNBism is a wise pronouncement from the mind of Arnbi.

SUPER-ARNBism is an extremely important rule about using information. There are only three.

ACKNOWLEDGMENTS

This brief book is about *No Bull Information*. Therefore, I shall not spend time thanking my first dog, Skipper, who was lost in a Thanksgiving blizzard of 1950. There are several groups of people who inspired and facilitated this book. First are my students at Penn State, the good ones, the not-so-good ones, and especially the ones whose horizons I helped to expand. Second are my faculty colleagues at Penn State many of whom helped me to develop my ideas. Third is the spirit of Penn State and I am <u>not</u> talking about athletics or Penn State's new slogan, "Penn State lives here." I am talking about the fact that, fundamentally, Penn State is a great university that encourages the open discussion of ideas even when controversial, unpleasant and/or insensitive. Finally, there are a few close friends who helped me when the book and I needed it most; you know who you are.

Listing the individuals who contributed is fraught with danger. Certainly, there will be omissions and a few who might prefer to disavow any connection with me or NBI. Here goes, listed alphabetically, without titles, degrees or the locations of any tattoos or body piercings.

Dick Aquila, Carl Bahm, Brenda Bane, F.S.J.S. Bane, Drew Bechtold, Jan Bendig-Tuznik, Mark Bratt, Sara Breese, Charlie Brock, Kristy Bunce, Meg Burke, Rachel Cacchione, Nate Carter, C.W. Cassinelli, Dave Christiansen, Heather Cole, Mauricio Cortes, Eric Corty, Allen Edwards, Diane Esser, Melcher Fobes, Wayne Francis, Lillie Gabreski, John Gamble, Chrissy Giuliano, Casey Graml, Nikki Gutgold, David Hagelin, David Hancock, Dan Hido, Sharon Hemminger, Stuart Hoffman, Jane Ingold, Alan James, Jonathan Kelley, Katherine Kelley, Tricia Kelley, Angie Kiesling, Albert Koers, Lauren Kolb, Agnes Ku, Charlotte Ku, Luke Laicia, Lorna Lloyd, George Looney, Jackie May, Ben Molstair, Mike Morris, Patti Mrozowski, Deb Nothum, Bell Pepalso, Mary Beth Pinto, Chuck Quadri, Tina Rapp, Mike Rebman, Martha Rodgers, Peter Rohn, Amanda Rooker, Mike Rutter, Natalie Rutter, Shirley Scott, Anna Scrimenti, Jess Scutella, Nicole Shoenberger, Henry Shuman, Rob Speel, Lynne Stout, Chris Strayer, Vedad Tabich, Toni Tan, Adam Terignoli, Margo Toulouse, Soledad Traverso, Rod Troester, Jorge Ubuntu, Aileen Wang, Mary Kay Williams, Kathryn Wolfe, Kim Young.

John Gamble
Erie, Pennsylvania
September 2014

CHAPTER 1

INTRODUCTION

ntroductions to books are difficult, especially when writing about a topic as broad as information. This is true for me. I have been a college professor for more than 30 years. I am convinced there are serious problems with the way information is presented and understood. This affects all Americans. I am writing for and to them.

At the most basic level, this book is about facts, basic units of information. I explain how facts are the building blocks of information and understanding. "Fact traps" are everywhere, many very subtle. As you'll see, understanding facts and what to do with them involves far more than recognizing and discarding misinformation. Often that is the easy part. Far more important is understanding facts, where they fit, and what to do with them.

1

On March 2, 1962, a basketball player scored 100 points in a single game. On the face of it, this seems like quite a big deal. But we must go further and put the fact into context. We need to know this was in the NBA, the premier professional basketball league in the world. The player, Wilt Chamberlain, was one of the greatest players who ever lived. This record has never been matched.[1] It's only in the context of this additional information that we can truly appreciate what an achievement Chamberlain accomplished in that game.

Americans need to be better equipped to evaluate the massive amounts of information bombarding us. A new type of information literacy must be developed for the Internet age. This is essential to the operation of our democracy and our free market economic system. We need a more astute citizenry, able to make more intelligent judgments if not to leap tall buildings in a single bound.[2] If we don't achieve this, competition in business will not work properly, election choices will be shortsighted, and our government will not be able to make tough decisions.

Thousands if not millions of people can participate in what I hope will become a mass movement that I call NBI—No-Bull Information. This will reduce the chances of bank bailouts, oil spills, elected officials who ignore scientific proof, and anonymous billionaires who spend obscene amounts of money on election campaigns. My goals might seem unrealistic and naïve. Once you read a bit further, I am confident you'll see this can work and you can be a part of it. The average American is smarter and more analytic than politicians, credit card companies, supermarkets, Super PACs, and TV shows seem to believe.

---

1   www.nba.com/history/wilt100_moments.html
2   While the message of this book is serious, I often am not. Your first indication is this irreverent reference to Superman's abilities.

The Information Age Demands New Strategies

Here's a central point: The US and other countries are constantly trying to decide what government should do. Should government merely get out of the way and let us decide how to spend our money? Or should government impose new laws and regulations to prevent crises like the financial meltdown of late 2008 or the massive Deepwater Horizon oil spill of spring 2010? What could and should have been done differently about the sloppy, poorly planned implementation of Obamacare in November of 2013? There is a huge debate about what, if anything, government should do to control costs and guarantee people have healthcare. Some—usually Republicans—believe the government should get out of the way and let the free market operate to control costs and raise the quality of healthcare.

Another heated discussion involves whether the government should enact measures that may help prevent atrocities like the 2012 massacre at Sandy Hook Elementary School in Connecticut. Can this be done without infringing on the 2nd Amendment? Does public safety take precedence over strict adherence to the right to keep and bear arms? There are few easy answers to questions like these.

If Americans demand clearer, more concise, less ambiguous information, government and our capitalist economic system will work better. As you will see, NBI concepts can be applied broadly, from how politicians answer questions to the price of toilet paper at Walmart. I want NBI to become a mass participatory sport to improve government and the marketplace. NBI can enable the economic and political systems to work better, the way a lubricant makes a machine run faster and more smoothly, resulting in fewer breakdowns.

How can an old college professor who has lived most of his adult life in an ivory tower write a book like this? Rather than duck this basic question, I will face it head-on with the top 11 (10 was just not enough) reasons why I could not possibly write a book about government, politics, and American capitalism aimed at a mass American audience. Obviously I can only write for academics. I intend to prove all 11 reasons are unfounded.

Top 11 Reasons NBI Cannot Possibly Work

11.   A 23-page article of mine published in the *Santa Clara Journal of International Law* in 2013 has 100 footnotes.

10.   Political science is boring for college students; it might destroy brain cells of the general public and make me vulnerable to lawsuits.

9.   These topics are too complex to explain to a broad audience; I will fail and will have to see a shrink whom I cannot afford until this book becomes a bestseller.

8.   A mere college professor cannot solve problems that have baffled, befuddled, and bedeviled brilliant presidents, governors, and members of Congress—and we all know how brilliant they are.

7.   I think I'm a pretty funny guy, but I'm past 60 and have never even been on network television or written for a popular magazine. Students do laugh at my jokes but perhaps only to try to get higher grades.

6.   I occasionally use Latin phrases. The US is a secular nation. Readers may think I am in the hip pocket of the Argentina-born pope, Jorge Mario Bergoglio.

5.   The NBI crusade will be drowned in a tsunami of bull-laden information.

4.   "For God's sake, Gamble"—(I talk to myself this way)—"drop the 'authoritative allocation of values' [see Chapter 3]. It's too deep for your audience!"

3. Americans love constant campaigning for president, so they will reject NBI.

2. Underneath it all, people really want bull-laden information, not NBI. It's like professional wrestling; people know it's fake but want to watch it anyway.

1. People are too self-conscious and timid to wear NBI hats and T-shirts in order to spread the word about NBI.

In a sense this book has been writing itself in my head for the last two decades. The deep recession that began in late 2007, the healthcare crisis, and the throw-the-bums-out attitude as the election of 2014 approaches show huge dissatisfaction and distrust. NBI can help change that.

For more than a quarter century I have endeavored to introduce college undergraduates to political science. This means I've tried to teach students about governments, what they are, how they are set up, what they claim to do, what they really do, and what they have no business doing. This is an important area of study, because it affects your life personally and directly. The huge budget deficit in the US and the oil spill in the Gulf of Mexico occurred because governments were doing some things poorly, often creating the illusion of effective regulation while ignoring many things that government alone can do. If enough people demand it, No-Bull Information can help government and the marketplace to achieve what is needed without overreaching.

What should government do? Careful! That is not an easy question to answer! Maybe government should prevent me from having a mortgage greater than the value of my house, but it should not tell me how to dress or where to worship. Maybe government should control how much money an individual or business gives to an election campaign, though the US Supreme Court seems to disagree.

We Americans are dealing with the most significant and complex array of issues at any time in our nearly 250-year history. I know what you're thinking—what about the Civil War, the Great Depression, and World War II? This time we have an intermingling of *what* we do and *how* we do it that is unmatched in history. It reminds me of Sir Winston Churchill's description of socialism—dealing with it is like unscrambling eggs. We have unimaginably changed modes of communication—cell phones and the Internet to name just two— that are so much faster and so different, they fundamentally alter both the information transmitted and the people involved in the transmission. Most of us are so immersed in this New Information Age, we forget how rapid and pervasive the change has been.

I've been a professor at Penn State for more than a third of a century. I clearly remember sitting on a bench in the center of my campus in Erie, Pennsylvania, on a warm day in April of 1981. The campus was alive with students rushing to get to their next class. I sat on the same bench in April of 2014. What are the principal differences? The students look about the same. Many more were smoking in 1981. Perhaps they walk faster today because the campus has grown. But the main difference is about 50% of the students are using their cell phones. And the change goes far beyond these funny little devices they hold up to their ears. Far fewer are talking to one another. Collisions among students are far more common and often affect old professors walking between buildings while thinking profound thoughts. This is just one tip of the Information Age iceberg. People want—or even demand—information that is fast, brief, and simple. Some information cannot be made fast, brief, and simple. We've got two choices—avoid or distort. I'm not promising to resolve all these problems, but I provide a range of tools for understanding, dealing with, and adapting to the Information Age. We can start modestly, perhaps by turning off our cell phones before entering public restrooms.

Questions for the Ages:

- What should government do?
- What can government do?
- How effectively does government do it?

CHAPTER 2

CONTEXT IS YOUR LIFELINE

As a political science professor, I can't help but write about politics. And politics certainly is essential to NBI. My interest in politics goes back as far as I can remember, to very early impressions of my father. He was a conservative, middle-America Republican who distrusted government, believing it usually got in the way of business efficiency and personal freedom and wasted money. Predictably, my father had been opposed to President Roosevelt, who served from 1933-45, and his New Deal.

I became politically aware at about the age of 10. I remember asking my father if Roosevelt's New Deal had helped the millions of people who were out of work and did not have money enough for food (unemployment exceeded 30 percent during the Depression, with far fewer safety nets—like unemployment insurance—than we have today).[3] My father's reaction was strange. He was an intelligent man, an engineer who rose to be vice president of engineering for a medium-sized company. He thought and reasoned like an engineer. He had looked for a job in 1933, at the depth of the Great Depression, found one, and worked his way up from apprentice toolmaker (at 19¢ an hour, about $6.80 today) to vice president 30 years later. He believed that if he could do it, anyone could.

I didn't recognize it at the time, but my father was demonstrating the strength of political party loyalties. From the time he was a kid, he had been told—perhaps "brainwashed" is not too strong a word—that the Republican Party was the best party for America. This made it impossible for him to accept, for example, that Franklin Roosevelt, a Democrat, may have been the best president for the America of the 1930s.

This demonstrates a vital, core point to NBI that you will confront many times in different contexts, including statistical sampling, infomercials, and family memories. We live in an era where there is more information more readily available to more people than at any time in history. For certain kinds of information, that is good. If I have forgotten the route to the salon of my favorite pedicurist, Mme. Laszlo, I can find it online in seconds. That's a good thing, since my feet and I rely on Mme. Laszlo.[4]

But there is so much information available that often it is impossible to distinguish between gems and junk. Perhaps this matters little if you buy a miracle apple peeler because of a slick infomercial. But it literally can be a life or death situation if you have a medical condition and turn to the Internet for advice. Some of the finest medical centers in the world have wonderful websites. There also are tens of thousands of quacks trying to get rich by selling unproven or useless cures for everything

---

3   Alter, Jonathan. *The Defining Moment: FDR's Hundred Days and the Triumph of Hope*. NY: Simon & Schuster Paperbacks, 2007. Print.

4   Remember—my message is serious, my writing often isn't.

from discolored toenails to cancer. And some of these ridiculous "cures" come in advertisements sponsoring serious TV programs or important, informative websites.

Much more problematic are situations where a fact or a few facts are correct in the sense that they really occurred but can be wildly unrepresentative and stunningly unusual. Here's an example many of you can identify with. My home, Erie, Pennsylvania, averages about 94 inches of snowfall per season. Occasionally, we really get blasted. On December 11, 1944, we received 26.5 inches of snow in 24 hours. There is another side to this weather coin. On Christmas Day, 1964, Erie recorded a maximum temperature of 66° on a sunny day. Both events made headlines in the newspaper, with too little explanation of how unusual they were. In fact, they were featured because they were the most unusual ever; that is what a "record" means.

This gets to the heart of NBI and to the dilemma we face. Facts may be accurate but still paint a distorted picture. A goal of NBI is not just getting our facts right but also understanding their context, how unusual they are, and how they fit in. For example, consider the "fact" of a black kid, born into poverty, raised by a single parent working a minimum wage job, and "educated" in a terrible inner city public city school system. Unfortunately, there are many of these "facts." However, we can find cases where a kid with this background goes to Harvard University as an undergraduate and then to Yale Law School. This is remarkable and a fulfillment of the American dream, but we must put this fact into context—it is highly unusual. It is far more likely that the first kid will wind up in jail.

Here is the essential balance NBI can help you to achieve. The sheer volume of information tends to turn off all contextual thinking. More than ever, people need serenity, security, and certainty of a kind that comes from individual experiences and personal memories often going back to childhood. NBI does not want to deny you these individual memories. You do not have to declare your grandfather a louse (even if he were). In fact, NBI, by placing information in a clearer and broader context, can be a tool to reconcile your personal experiences with the wider world you live in.

The grandeur many people can achieve comes from intimate, individual life experiences that shaped them. The first step is accepting that they are part of you. My father and his experience living in the shadow of the Great Depression are a part of me. In fact, ripples of the Great Depression continue into a third generation. I see them in my son. I can love my father and my grandfather while understanding that their views, opinions, and attitudes may have limited meaning beyond how they shaped me and a few others. NBI is a process that can help you to accept your past—in fact, you can use it as a springboard rather than a roadblock to functioning in our information-dense world.

A technique I've adapted from decades of college teaching is one that I call Rx3—Rewind, Reveal, and Rant. While lecturing or just talking with students, often I express something less clearly than I'd like, because I assume that the students have a certain body of knowledge that they lack. Rather than continue down an unproductive path, I stop, say "rewind," and start over with an improved approach.

Here are the three R's:

- "Rewind" because I'm pausing and going backwards a bit;
- "Reveal" because it is a point that needs deeper discussion; and
- "Rant" because there sometimes is an element of preachy anger in my message.

You can look forward to six Rx3s in this book. Some are intended to be provocative, others just informative. I hope some will amuse you. Here's the first:

Rx3 #1: A Smidgen of Latin

I never took Latin, in part because I did not go to Catholic school. But my research specialty is International Law, a field in which I have published scores of articles. You can't write about International Law and avoid Latin completely, so I've developed the habit of using some in my other writing, including in this book. I like it as long as it is not overly cumbersome. Four terms to get you started (and maybe impress your friends):

i.e. = that is (don't confuse it with e.g.)

e.g. = for example (don't confuse it with i.e.)

sic = an abbreviation in Latin for "as such" or "thus." It is used to show that the preceding word or phrase is written exactly as intended in spite of the fact it may appear to be wrong.

Tabula Rasa = "scraped tablet" or less literally "clean slate." I confess to using the expression in part because so many people get it wrong, often writing "Tabula Rosa," which makes no sense. "Rosa" in Latin means the flower but metamorphosized into the color red in some of the languages that developed from Latin.

Back to my political roots—I don't want to sell my father short. I have considered myself a feminist since I was 10, when my mother told me that she graduated from Allegheny College, a prestigious liberal arts college, at the age of 20 as an economics major, with straight A's and highest honors. She tried to find a job in the summer of 1939 and was told she would have to learn to type to be considered for any employment!

Both of my parents were subjected to a constant barrage of questions from me and generally had the patience of Job, a quality that I tried to repeat with my son. One of the thousands of questions I asked my father was whether there were women engineers. He said, "Women don't have ability in those areas." He didn't dare reveal this opinion to my mother! A couple of years later, my father came home from his job as manager of engineering at a medium-sized company. We were having one of our frequent dinner-table discussions when he said, "I need to admit I was wrong. I spent the day with a group of engineers visiting from Germany. One of them was a woman. She was excellent." He had changed his mind about women engineers on the spot and permanently.

My father realized that his notion that women couldn't do engineering was wrong, but his changed opinion was based on only one counter example. That certainly was better than denying the fact that this German woman was a talented engineer. But it apparently did not occur to my father that he had an obligation to help women succeed as engineers. Just as he was, we are all a product of the time and circumstances in which we live.

Later, as an undergraduate student at the College of Wooster (in north central Ohio, not in Massachusetts) and as a graduate student at the University of Washington (in Seattle, not in St. Louis or DC), my interest in politics broadened and was recalibrated. The fact that I'm curious about almost everything and a good observer and cataloger of information, coupled with teaching tens of thousands of students, sowed the seeds for this book.

But back to NBI. The real need for NBI results from our complex world, where generally accurate messages and blatant lies both fail to adhere to high standards for information. The mess in which we find ourselves has few needles of accuracy in a growing haystack of information. People do not know whom to believe, so they assume everyone is lying or at least misleading, that all government is bad, most businesses are corrupt, and that almost everyone has an axe to grind.

Valid Messages–but Serious Flaws

Exaggerating good things makes it harder to recognize crap.

The three examples below were carefully selected to illustrate a vitally important point about information that does not measure up to the highest NBI standards. All three are knowledgeable people and/ or good products that did not present (and should have presented) information in a clear, direct, and understandable way. These examples remind me of star professional athletes who occasionally exaggerate their already exemplary accomplishments.

Case #1: During the 2012 presidential campaign, President Barack Obama said, "After 30 years of inaction, we raised fuel standards so that by the middle of the next decade, cars and trucks will go twice as far on a gallon of gas."[5]

On September 6, 2012, President Obama gave a speech at the Democratic National Convention in Charlotte, North Carolina, during which he made the announcement I quoted above. But how accurate was this statement? In 2011 the Obama administration did issue regulations that set an average fuel efficiency goal of 54.5 miles per gallon, to be reached by the 2025 model year (the goal for 2011 was 27.6 miles per gallon).[6]

But was there 30 years of inaction? In 2007, President Bush signed the Energy Independence and Securities Act which, according to the Environmental Protection Agency's website, sought to "increase efficiency of products, buildings, and vehicles" as well as "improve

---

5   http://www.politifact.com/truth-o-meter/statements/2012/sep/10/barack-obama/
     obama-fuel-standards-inaction/
6   Ibid.

vehicle fuel economy."[7] One section of the act states, "The Secretary shall prescribe a separate average fuel economy standard … for each model year beginning with model year 2011 to achieve a combined fuel economy average for model year 2020 of at least 35 miles per gallon."[8]

This law clearly was the foundation for Obama's increased fuel economy regulations. Those who value the environment agree that increased fuel economy standards are a positive step. Credit is due to the Obama administration for working with automobile companies while extending the regulations and setting a higher bar for fuel economy. However, it was inaccurate for President Obama to claim sole responsibility for this accomplishment.

Case # 2: Major Garrett reported on the *CBS Evening News* that a new energy plan "could reduce carbon-based pollution by 500 tons."

Major Garrett is the chief White House correspondent for CBS News, and the information he provides is usually clear, concise, and of high quality. Following the 2013 presidential inauguration, Garrett was asked to explain how President Obama intended to deal with global warming. His response did not adhere to high NBI standards. Garrett stated that rather than attempting to push new legislation through Congress, Obama may ask the Environmental Protection Agency (EPA) to create a plan that would broaden the scope of the Clean Air Act. The new plan would include limitations on the carbon emissions of existing power plants and not just target new power plants—"a move that environmentalists say could reduce carbon-based pollution by 500 tons by the year 2020."[9] There are many problems with this statement.

---

7   http://www2.epa.gov/laws-regulations/summary-energy-independence-and-security-act

8   http://www.gpo.gov/fdsys/pkg/BILLS-110hr6enr/pdf/BILLS-110hr6enr.pdf

9   Pelley, Scott, and Major Garrett. "Obama's Next Moves on Climate Change, Immigration?" *CBS Evening News*. CBS. 22 Jan. 2013. Cbsnews.com.

- First, Garrett is citing "environmentalists," which is problematic for a couple of reasons: He did not state which environmental groups this information came from, and environmentalists have a vested interest in reducing carbon emissions (indeed, we all do) and therefore may not be the most reliable source of information on this subject.

- The second problem with the statement is the claim that this plan could reduce carbon emissions by 500 tons. Not only is it impossible for most people to comprehend the idea of 500 tons of airborne carbon, but we don't know how significant a reduction this would be as a percent of total carbon output.

- The third problem is this would be a 500-ton reduction "by the year 2020." This is tricky, and something you should look out for. The 500-ton reduction grabs your attention because it's the first figure you hear, and it sounds significant, but this figure is a reduction over a seven-year period, making the information sensational but extremely hard to interpret.

Case # 3: Toyota announced that "80% of Toyotas sold in the last 20 years are still on the road today."[10]

While it is true that Toyota vehicles tend to be reliable and last longer than most other brands (no, I do not own stock in the company, but you should ask that question), the statistic provided here is intentionally misleading. It is true that 80% of Toyota vehicles from the past 20 years

CBS Interactive Inc. Web. 25 Jan. 2013. <http://www.cbsnews.com/video/watch/?id=50139506n>.

10   Toyota of Albany, Georgia. Advertisement. *YouTube*. Google, 29 Mar. 2010. Web. 25 Jan. 2013. <https://www.youtube.com/watch?v=GmdSKQYyC2M>.

are still on the road. So what's the catch? Well, Toyota sales in the US doubled since 1992.[11]

Time period	Toyotas sold	Percent of 20-year total
1992-1996	4.6 million	16 percent
1997-2001	6.6 million	22 percent
2002-2006	9.1 million	31 percent
2007-2011	9.1 million	31 percent

Look at the table above. Toyota sold 29.4 million vehicles total from 1992-2011. Only 2.5% of those were sold in 1992, and the first five-year period accounted for 16% of total sales through 2011. Here is the reason the statement is technically accurate: Compared to Toyota's more recent sales numbers, far fewer Toyotas were sold from 1992-96, so the majority of the vehicles sold in that time period can be sitting in a junk yard and Toyota can still claim that 80% of its vehicles sold in the last 20 years are still on the road. In fact, only about 36 percent of Toyota's 16- to 20-year-old passenger cars are still on the road.[12] Later I'll explain much more about sampling and statistics to enable you to deal better with such information.

The need for higher standards for information—NBI—will help people to cut through the crap and assess the merits of politicians' statements, the price of bread, and that agreement for your new mortgage. NBI is like a corrective lens than can help you to see the complex world more clearly and understand your choices.

Your eyes will adjust, and the bull will become evident.

---

11   "Toyota Reports." The Free Library. Web. & Toyota.com
12   DesRosiers, Dennis. "Observations: Twenty-Five Years of Vehicle Longevity."
     DesRosiers Automotive Reports. DesRosiers Automotive Consultants Incorporated,
     15 Dec. 2010. Web. 25 Jan. 2013. <http://www.fleetbusiness.com/pdf/DD7.pdf>.

My focus is on information, information of all kinds that Americans deserve but too often are denied. I want to inspire hundreds of thousands of Americans to demand more accurate, understandable, consistent information, whether that information comes from a politician, your local XtraThrifteeMart, your Honda dealer, or from those unbelievable television infomercials. The concept is quite simple but it can make a huge difference. If we, the people—yes, in a way this can help to create a more perfect union—refuse to buy products, watch news programs, or vote for candidates unless they adhere to the high NBI standards explained here, we can help to improve both the government and the free market economic system of America.

Rx3 #2: Infomercials

I am renaming infomercials "very long commercials using pseudo experts disguised as experts recorded in front of audiences that would clap enthusiastically at the sight of crabgrass growing." Let's call them "Velcupedes" for short. Putting aside the absurdness of most Velcupedes, they violate more NBI principles than anything else I can think of. The first principle violated is the name. Once you buy into and begin to use a name based on misinformation, you're likely to lose the battle. The lesson of not being suckered by a name is important in many aspects of NBI, so fight back and chortle when comedians start to talk about Velcupedes. I don't want to condemn all infomercials; there probably are a few good apples in the barrel, but be damned careful which apples you eat.

CHAPTER 3

AAoV: A (DIGESTIBLE) MOUTHFUL

n order to understand how NBI can help decode our chaotic politics, we have to begin with some fundamental concepts. Several years ago, while walking my dog, Belle, at 6 a.m., it occurred to me NBI and its link to government might seem more complex and mysterious than need be. Specific examples are needed to understand any concept, so fasten your seatbelts—here we go.

Political scientists often explain governments and their actions by talking about the authoritative allocation of values (AAoV), a concept important to NBI. Let's break down this mouthful into its three elements.

- **"Authoritative" or "authority"** refers to the legal right to do something. Some people believe that governments are the only institutions in society that have authority since they alone have the right to tell us what to do. This is an oversimplification. Parents have some right to tell their children what to do. As a college professor, I have some authority over my students, at least within the sphere of the classes they take from me but perhaps not enough authority to make them take their baseball hats off or—perish the thought—not use cell phones in class.

- Moving next to **"allocation,"** we must deal with government's real-world use of authority. What does government do to exercise its authority? Does government warn us, ask us nicely, bribe us, shoot us, threaten us on TV and the Internet, explain in schools why we should obey it? The answer can be "yes" to all of these.

- **"Values"** are the behaviors government thinks it should allocate, i.e., make or at least encourage us to do. Values can include the following:
  - protecting us from foreign invasion
  - assuring food safety
  - encouraging safe driving of our automobiles
  - requiring failsafe blowout protection on oil wells
  - keeping those under 18 years old from buying cigarettes
  - preventing child abuse
  - protecting the American flag from disrespect
  - requiring Americans to buy health insurance
  - assuring freedom of religion
  - protecting the right to privacy

This list could go on. It is constantly evolving. There are enormous disagreements about how much government should do and at what point it should stop trying to allocate certain values.

 AAoV is worth the effort!

Saving Bambi's Life

I've tried to teach the authoritative allocation of values to thousands of students. It is not easy, so I am going to enlist the help of Bambi, that iconic character from the 1942 Disney movie. In case you had no childhood or suppressed it due to an acquired taste for venison, Bambi was a loveable fawn who was orphaned soon after birth. The name "Bambi" now is common in the English language, often used as a synonym for any deer, especially young ones.

I live in northwestern Pennsylvania about 35 miles from the Ohio line close to the south shore of Lake Erie. If you are geographically challenged, draw a line from Boston to Chicago—I'm close to the midpoint. Deer hunting is a religion in this part of the world; deer seem to be everywhere. Many children are given hunting rifles from the tooth fairy when they lose their first baby tooth (slight exaggeration).

The proudest moment for many parents (usually fathers) is taking their son—increasingly daughters too—deer hunting. The local newspaper prints dozens of pictures of proud parents and their children with their first successful kill. The typical picture shows a parent and a child grinning from ear to ear and the deer draped over the hood of a pickup truck.

My corner of Pennsylvania has thousands of deer, especially just before deer hunting season starts in late fall. I have gone deer hunting twice in the last 30 years—never with a gun, both times, involuntarily, with my automobile. Pennsylvania has a huge number of deer-related car accidents. My first collision with a deer nearly destroyed my car. Much worse is when a car swerves to avoid a deer, crosses the median line, and collides head-on with a truck coming in the opposite direction. Bear with me; the connection between NBI and driving soon will be clear.

I love cars, took my driving test 48 hours after my 16th birthday, failed it, passed it four days later and had my first accident that same evening. After this minor accident, I became a cautious and careful driver although really impatient with inconsiderate behavior on the part of the 200 million other drivers in the US. After about six months, my father thought I was getting the hang of driving and let me drive to the closest city, Erie, about 40 miles north of Meadville where I was born and grew up. I already knew the route from riding with my parents dozens of times. It is a relatively good two-lane road with a couple of little towns in between the "megalopoli" of Meadville (population about 18,000) and Erie (population about 100,000).

 What a transition!
NBI → Arnbi → Bambi

Because I have been doing the Meadville to Erie drive as long as I can remember and happened to get a job at Penn State's Behrend College in Erie, I have made this round trip at least 1,000 times, and I have seen many, many deer along the route. In fact, it was on this route that I had both "deer hunting" accidents. Many of my friends have hit deer along this route. Accidents involving deer cost millions of dollars in increased car insurance premiums not to mention the unforgettable experience of looking a deer in the eye, 18 inches away, as it bounces off the fender of the car and momentum carries its dying body across your windshield.

How does the authoritative allocation of values relate to this deer menace? Since the deer situation endangers public safety and occasionally even kills people, doesn't the government have an obligation to do something, to allocate values? In this case the values should include preventing or at least reducing the number of accidents and deaths. But what can or should be done? Is it clear what the government should do? Since the natural balance of species has been irreparably changed by more than 250 years of human activity in the region (e.g., the elimination of natural predators such as wolves), the deer population would increase significantly in the absence of a deer population management strategy.[13]

Pennsylvania both allows hunting to keep the deer population from increasing out of control and strictly regulates it to ensure that the deer population is not decimated for future hunters. The game commission creates its population management strategy "to increase, decrease, or stabilize ... trends" in the deer population.[14] We've got competing values and have to decide which to allocate. Many Pennsylvania hunters view their right to deer hunting to be fundamental, just behind freedom of speech. A state legislator who advocated decimating the deer population to increase road safety and reduce costs probably would be defeated in the next election.

Furthermore, although deer are a nuisance to drivers, farmers, loggers, and homeowners, hunting is important to the state's overall economy, especially in small communities. Hunters spend $1.6 billion[15] in Pennsylvania annually. The money the state receives from the sale of hunting licenses and federal taxes on hunting-related goods such as ammunition and guns goes directly toward wildlife management (not just deer management).[16]

I don't want to beat the dead deer much longer; we should let Bambi's mom rest in deer heaven. When allocating values related to hunting, Pennsylvania has to strike a balance between increasing road safety and preventing deer-related property damage versus protecting the hunting culture and the local economy. The point is the authoritative allocation

---

13   An Evaluation of Deer Management Options. The Wildlife Society and the
     Northeast Deer Technical Committee. May 2009.

14   Rosenberry, Christopher, Jeannine T. Fleegle, and Bret D. Wallingford.
     Monitoring Deer Populations in Pennsylvania. *PA Game Commission*. Jan. 2011.

15   http://articles.mcall.com/2013-12-17/sports/mc-outdoor-
     ramblings-12162013-20131217_1_pennsylvania-economic-impact-businesses

16   US Department of the Interior, Fish and Wildlife Service, and US Department of
     Commerce, US Census Bureau. 2006 National Survey of Fishing, Hunting, and
     Wildlife-Associated Recreation.

of values is tricky, complicated stuff and, especially in a democracy, is limited by the will of the people or more accurately by those people who are especially concerned about certain issues. It might be cheaper for Pennsylvania simply to eliminate all deer, but that would be politically impossible and ecologically undesirable. Many people will not accept certain actions even if the value allocated is positive.

Something Has to Give

Entire books have been written about the authoritative allocation of values.[17] Judgments about the allocation change drastically over time. In the case of my four-legged Bambi friends in Pennsylvania, what value is state government allocating—safe roads? The right to hunt? The right to drive? Sixty years ago smoking was permitted in virtually all interior spaces in the United States, including college classrooms and hospital rooms. Now it is prohibited virtually everywhere and in California even outside within 20 feet of the exterior doors to public buildings. Society has struck a new balance and people generally have accepted a change in how a value—protecting people from secondhand smoke—has been allocated.

If people don't accept the new balance, eventually something has to give. This occurred during Prohibition where the sale of alcoholic beverages was banned from 1919 until 1933. This was a complete failure. It created a huge illegal, underground economy to meet demand for alcoholic beverages. Some studies found that consumption of alcoholic beverages increased during Prohibition. Eventually attitudes changed so President Franklin Roosevelt could sign the repeal of Prohibition in 1933.

Back to the situation in 2014. Huge deficits, multiple wars in the Middle East, and an increased fear of global warming have created a new climate with many calling for much more governmental action and

---

17   Easton, David. *A Framework for Political Analysis*. Englewood Cliffs: Prentice-Hall, 1965 and Easton, David. *The Analysis of Political Structure*. Routledge, 1990.

regulation. But there is a countertrend seen in the Tea Party that believes government often is clueless and should do and spend much less. This is heavy-duty authoritative allocation of values. Part of the difficulty can be traced to January 1981. President Ronald Reagan, in his first inaugural address, said: "Government is not the solution to our problem. Government is the problem."[18] There is some truth to President Reagan's statement. Many of us are frustrated as hell when government seems out of touch, creating mindless regulations, increasing its own size, and stifling innovation and creativity.

One of my favorite examples is that of French President Charles de Gaulle who, reflecting on the overregulated French state, wrote "How can you govern a country which has 246 varieties of cheese?"[19] President de Gaulle's statement shows the dilemma. Most Americans believe government should not set and enforce standards for 246 kinds of cheese. But should government enforce safety standards so people do not get sick from eating cheese? What about exact rules for what can be called "cheese"? You can see the complexity. Where would most Americans draw the line?

Government must play a major role in allocating values. However, we must carefully assess what government can and should do or the result will be wasteful, obtrusive government and, eventually, government that is neither respected nor obeyed. What happens when millions of parents tell their children that government is the problem and wastes our money and provides precious little in return? The real answer is harder to understand and to teach to our children—that we have to

18 Reagan, Ronald. "Inaugural Address." Address. 1981 Presidential Inauguration. United States Capitol, Washington, DC, 20 Jan. 1981. *Reagan Foundation*. The Ronald Reagan Presidential Foundation & Library. 8 Jan. 2013.
19 *Les Mots du General [de Gaulle]*. Ernest Mignon. *Librairie Artheme Fayard*: 1962. I love France, but to American eyes it seems overregulated (too many values being allocated), e.g., stores are only allowed to have sales twice per year at times specified by the government.

assess carefully what government should do, how it should act, and when it should act.

Rx3 #3 America Is the Greatest Country Ever

Many Americans arrogantly proclaim the United States is the best in the world or best ever in virtually every way. This tendency is not new, but it has become more extreme in recent years. I love my country and am very proud of many of the things we have accomplished, e.g., great scientific discoveries, widespread acceptance of people from all parts of the world, and providing much individual freedom. But we are not the best at everything. To say so is not anti-American. We have completely mangled President Theodore Roosevelt's wise advice: "Speak softly and carry a big stick." Far too often today, we speak too quickly, too loudly, with too little knowledge and far too little forethought about the use of the array of big sticks we possess. A good example is the categorical statement "the US has the best healthcare system in the world." That may be true for the very wealthy but not for the majority of Americans. We spend much more per person than any country in the world, and we do not get the best results. Germany, Britain, and Canada each spends less and gets better overall outcomes. Further, if we are concerned about the government becoming too powerful (as we should be), sweeping statements about US superiority should be minimized. So let's show a little humility before trumpeting our superiority. And let's avoid the statement, "I'll never apologize for the US." Countries, like people, are mperfect. When either screws up, an apology often is in order. Why? Because it's the right thing to do, it helps us to get along with other countries and, most important, it's one of the best paths to improvement.

Proclaiming something to be the best reduces the likelihood that it's true, like the corner store with the "World's Best Coffee."

My ambitious goal is to get tens of thousands of Americans to follow certain principles and demand NBI. If enough people do this, government's job will be easier. Clearer information can reduce the pressure for government to do too much. This will make both the liberal Left and conservative Right[20] unhappy. The Left wants government to do more and will resent that NBI reduces the need for certain governmental actions. The Right wants the government to do less and will resent that NBI will blunt their assertion that all regulation is bad and that government screws up everything it touches. When both the extreme Left and extreme Right disagree with me, that's a sign I'm onto something.

I have covered many complex ideas in a way that I hope is understandable and strikes a responsive chord. Now I will turn to specific strategies for NBI that can be applied in a number of different situations.

Below are your first two ARNBisms. Take a minute to savor them and understand their power.

My students often complain about the complexity of the concepts I am trying to teach them. I tell them that simplicity is great; it feels good and provides security and peace, but much of the modern world is not simple. Wishing and longing for simplicity does not bring it about. Quite the contrary, if you try to force simplicity onto a complex problem, you'll probably make things worse.

---

20 For those who are not immersed in politics —"Left" generally means the belief that government is a positive, should be more active, and that, generally, actions like regulation and more spending are good. "Conservative" usually means government should tax less and, generally, do less. Prosperity and freedom are achieved by limiting or reducing government.

ARNB SM — Too bad, but "simple" is a square peg that seldom fits into the round hole that is our modern world.

There is an old saying: "It's not a black or white situation." This expression has a bad and often misunderstood reputation. To many, it produces an image of gray where most principles have been compromised, but this does not have to be the case. Although black-and-white interpretations of real-world issues are often much easier to understand and accept, such interpretations rarely produce constructive dialogue and effective solutions. We tend to observe things in black-and-white terms in order to simplify life's most complex issues in ways that make them easier to deal with. Reality comes in many shades of gray. There can be beauty in gray, but also frustration.

NBI can make it much easier to see the gray. Maybe the "beauty of gray" is too much to ask, but at least more people will understand that gray exists. Gray is about finding the correct balance, e.g., not repeating overregulation but establishing a framework where we decide what values government should allocate and how to do it best. It also is about balancing individuals' actions against the broader good of society. This is not European-style socialism, as some have charged; it is nothing more or less than living in our modern, complex world.

Rx3 #4: Acronyms

This is an important Rx3 since I've been practicing what I'm warning against — mea maxima culpa (Latin for "my most serious fault"). I am talking, of course, about acronyms. We all use them, often without realizing it. Examples: FBI (Federal Bureau of Investigation), UN (United Nations), IOC (International Olympic Committee), CNN (Cable News Network). I've admitted I'm a car nut. How many Americans who drive BMWs know that

BMW stands for Bayerische Motoren Werke or Bavarian Motors Works in English? Many times we forget what they stand for or even that they are acronyms. But the real problem is acronyms have almost magical power, making those who use them seem like influential insiders with status and knowledge. Knowing and using many acronyms can be a characteristic of expert, knowledgeable, powerful insiders. But acronyms can be a diversion used by clueless individuals trying to sneak something past you, like an Army private donning a general's uniform and expecting to be treated like a general. If you want more proof just look at the TV commercials whose main feature is an acronym no one has heard of pronounced in a deep, solemn voice. Be very careful of acronyms including (you've guessed it) NBI

A warning about acronyms from one: be suspicious of acronyms. Never hesitate to ask what they mean.

Stone-Skipping and Deep Thinking

In order to be proficient in NBI, you must learn to think longer term and more analytically. You need to recognize and control one type of prejudice that is an essential part of being human: assuming that your limited, individual life circumstances are accurate indicators of the broader human experience. This is part of the sampling problem covered later. Everybody has been bombarded by "traditional wisdom," from schoolyard friends to our grandparents. Some information we received was accurate, some harmless, some pretty intelligent, some dead wrong, and most oversimplified.

NBI requires that we look beyond these prejudices (note that "prejudice" comes from "prejudge") as part of thinking more analytically. I don't want to take all the fun out of life, but it is necessary to discipline yourself to step out of your experiential shell and realize that even what your beloved grandfather told you might not have been accurate. Once you see beyond the box, you can behave like a chess master or big-city taxi driver who naturally thinks many moves ahead.

I believe analytical thinking can complement other aspects of your life. I'll personalize this with a wonderful memory from my youth. Imagine yourself as a seven-year-old kid on the shore of a beautiful pond on a perfect July day. You want to skip a stone across a pond and remember your granddad (granddad is my memory—substitute your favorite relative) showing you how much fun skipping stones can be. Preserve that fond memory when your granddad, or whoever, introduced you to the wonder and amazement of picking up a simple flat stone and discovering that if thrown at exactly the correct speed and angle, it could defy nature and bounce across the surface of the pond. Stones don't bounce on water. Take that Isaac Newton! My granddad showed me they could.

Memories like this remind us of simpler times of absolute truths. You can keep those memories. They are what makes you *you*. But now as an NBI-seeking adult, you can expand and think on different levels without having to give up those granddad stone-skipping memories.

Let's expand on this example of stone skipping. Yes, my grandfather, Carl Sunderbrink, really did introduce me to stone skipping. Granddad— as I called him—was a good man, a kind man, but he was not perfect. This example shows how you can embrace your past, imperfections and all, and build on it without letting it immobilize you. Broaden your thinking to the entire range and context of stone-skipping, including:

- when you first discovered the act of stone-skipping
- who taught you (substitute your equivalent of my granddad)
- how you learned to select the perfect stone
- realizing that skipping stones is hard on a windy day
- on some days were there so many people skipping stones that you had to compete for the best stone

- on some days were there so many stone throws you could not follow your own eddy
- was there one day when you had unbelievable luck: perfect pond, perfect stone, perfect throw
- follow your eddy; does it ever really end
- what really made this memory so great—the stone-skipping or memories of time spent with a beloved relative? Can the two memories be separated?
- what is the overall effect of "relocating" thousands of stones—destruction of the pond
- should stone-skipping be regulated—perish the thought—allocating a value so there are places from which to build future memories

I don't want to ruin what might be as fond a memory for you as it is for me, but it is possible to retain the simple beautiful memory while using it as a pathway to analytical thinking. In many ways, NBI becomes possible when we understand the people, places, and yes, prejudices of our past. That understanding–via NBI–permits improvement without denying your past.

Now let me introduce you to three of the most important points of this book. When any of these rules are broken, Arnbi cannot help but cry. Because they are so important, these are not just ARNBisms. A new image is needed to convey their importance:

SUPER-ARNBism #1

Balance your interests against those of seven billion others.

NBI is a way to handle that most frustrating of all battles: you against the world.

You are an individual. You deserve respect, freedom, and the recognition that you are different from everyone else.	BUT	You must share planet earth with seven billion others. Your uniqueness requires respect for others as they strive for happiness, freedom, and security.

SUPER-ARNBism #2

Facts are necessary but they must be put into context (PUTFiC).

Getting the facts right is the first step, but then you must put them into context. A fact: On December 25, 1982 the temperature in Chicago reached 64° but . . .

SUPER-ARNBism #3
Vested interests are everywhere—recognize them!

Be alert to basic, underlying motives: Selling you a car? Getting your vote? Taking your money?

Now that you've gotten through the preceding material on your path to NBI, we must delve further into an area many people find terrifying: numbers! But before you decide to incinerate this book and dwell only in an ideal world of absolute and simple truths, read the next chapter. I promise I won't make you do any algebra or calculus, and what you'll learn could save you money and frustration in the real world. Try it. I can't promise you'll love it, but I'm quite sure you'll be better for it.

CHAPTER 4

LEARN TO LIVE WITH NUMBERS
OR THEY'LL BAMBOOZLE YOU

N ow I venture into the most difficult material in this book, but
it's material that cannot be ignored.

I've always had a pretty good head for numbers. I can still
do arithmetic faster than my 28-year- old son, who recently received
his Ph.D. in physics. I took a lot of math as an undergraduate at the
College of Wooster. Many of my hundred or so publications employ
some statistics.

Because I teach many introductory courses open to college students
from any major, I have a pretty good sense for how uncomfortable
college students are with numbers, and what I see frightens me. Many of
the college students I encounter today—and those at Penn State are

better than the national average—are almost allergic to numbers. The reasons are complicated, no doubt including how math is taught, attitudes towards it, unfortunate, inaccurate stereotypes (e.g., girls can't do math and science), and the overuse of calculators and computers.

 Allergy to numbers can be treated with bed rest and this book.

The situation has deteriorated over the last 30 years. What follows is almost a tutorial on concepts relating to numbers and quantities that are essential for active involvement in your new favorite participatory sport: carrying the banner for NBI to every corner of America. Some of you already are comfortable with numbers; this can be your chance to help others who break into a cold sweat when confronted with a square root sign or anything more complicated than a simple calculation.

You don't have to become a math whiz, but you need to understand enough not to be deceived. You may gain new confidence in your NBI crusade simply by reviewing a few concepts about numbers and quantities so you can activate the power of an important NBI tool—the statement, "I don't understand; please explain." When used properly, this simple tactic can plow through piles of bull-laden information, stopping the purveyors of bull in their tracks. But most people need to have a basic knowledge of some numeric concepts to get the nerve to use "I don't understand" more effectively.

This is not the place to reteach counting let alone delve into statistics, but you have to remember a few things many of us learned before we were 15 years old. This is more necessary than ever because of the Internet age in which we live. Don't stop reading this book to watch MTV, Comedy Central, or The Weather Channel—I am not going to go into anything deep. In fact, this is so simple you probably understand much of it already.

Let me begin with two important concepts essential to NBI: constant dollar price and percentages/percentage points.

Constant Dollar Pricing

In June 1967 I graduated from the College of Wooster in Ohio. I begged my parents to let me accompany two college friends on an eight-week trip to Europe. OK, by "beg" I mean convince them to pay for the trip. My father, a kind man who, like an entire generation was permanently changed by the Great Depression, wanted his kids to have all the advantages our income level could provide. So my parents footed the bill for an airplane ticket for me. The best deal available through a travel agency was $560 roundtrip from New York City to Frankfurt, Germany. I was thrilled when the travel agency told me they had gotten enough passengers so the price could be reduced to $490. But you cannot directly compare 40-year-old prices with those of today. That $490 in 1967 equates to about $3,500 in 2014!

This has implications beyond buying plane tickets, sunscreen, and Starbucks coffee. Politicians, commentators and, yes, college professors, often try to make a point by using figures not adjusted for buying power. Some of the most egregious examples are claims made by both major parties that sound like this hypothetical example:

> "You must vote for the Democratic presidential candidate, Senator Happierdaze. After more than seven years in the White House, Republican President Notaclue has increased the national debt by almost as much as all previous presidents combined."

This kind of statement is dangerously misleading because, technically, in actual dollar figures, it might be true, but it does not account for huge changes in buying power over the years. For example, if President Woodrow Wilson had incurred a national debt of $1 billion in 1915, that would equate to $24 billion today. This example hits closer to home:

Approximate Price of a Loaf of Bread (in actual money spent at the time)

1813	1913	2013
1¢	6¢	$2.00

Percentages and Percentage Points– Great Tools if Used Properly

Only one more excursion into numbers, and we're done with this section.[21] Kids learn percentages very early in school and for obvious reasons. If the price of a watermelon goes up $1, that might be a 20% increase. A one dollar price increase in the price of a pair of high-end Nike shoes would be less than 1%, practically insignificant. Percentages are essential to interpreting many kinds of information. One of my favorite (yes, hypothetical) senators, Mortimer Govsbad from the great state of Alabama, said the following:

"It's a travesty. The country has the largest deficit in history, and the Democrats want to spend $20 million investigating procurement fraud in the weapons systems the Department of Defense buys. These are good, hard-working Americans trying to defend our country. Instead of thanking them, we investigate and waste even more of the taxpayers' hard-earned money."

This is not the place to discuss Pentagon procurement—there is plenty of room for improvement, but the $20 million Govsbad is complaining about has to be understood in context. It is less than one

---

21 My mother, who lived until almost 93, is largely responsible for my fussiness about grammar. Every time I write or say "done" I hear her saying "meat gets done, people get finished"—sorry, Mom, can't meat get finished?

dollar for each quarter million dollars the Pentagon spends, a portion so low it can't easily be understood even as a percentage. Try this instead. Compared to the Pentagon's entire budget of about $700 billion, Govsbad's $20 million is like taking an eyedropper and squeezing one drop into a two-liter bottle. Remember this image (I'll expand on it later). Furthermore, the $20 million has the potential to save much more money than it costs.

The senator is taking advantage of the fact that $20 million seems like a huge sum to the average person and it is, since it's almost 300 times the average annual income of an American household. There are many other number distortion games that people like Senator Govsbad play. For example, he might say these proposed new programs will cost a trillion dollars, slightly more than the total US spending on defense this year. If you read the fine print, you'll see that the trillion dollars is an estimate of what will be spent over 10 years. I am not saying that the Pentagon gets too much money or that the trillion dollars is wisely spent. We should demand our leaders use figures that are as accurate as possible and are presented in a fair, commonsense[22] way.

Politicians' speeches, drug company ads, professors, and so forth often cite figures that seem huge when you only see the raw figures, such as $129 million of government funding for a failed green energy company. This figure is the equivalent of 1.5 drops into a two-liter bottle, assuming the volume of the bottle signifies the entire budget. Percentages can be a great tool for many kinds of information, such as the fact that in 2013 the federal government raised revenues totaling about 20 percent or one-fifth of our whole economy.

However, with small proportions, we need another approach: Arnbi to the rescue with Drops in a Bottle or DiBs. For example, what is $1 billion? A billion is a thousand million. It does not help much to write

---

22　Astute readers will see the problem with the word "commonsense." NBI practices what it preaches and exposes the meaning of "commonsense." See Chapter 3.

$1,000,000,000 or to say the annual income of an American family (about $50,000) would be half of 1/100 of 1% of a billion dollars. Instead of using these incomprehensible numbers, I decided the following examples would be easier to understand and visualize:

- a two-liter (or two quart) bottle. They are everywhere, for juice or soda (pop).
- a gently squeezed drop of water from an eyedropper. Everybody has used an eyedropper. There are about 40,000 drops in our bottle.

It takes 40,000 drops.

No, I'm not crazy—at least not in this case. DiBs are an excellent way to understand and visualize extremely small parts. Here are a couple of examples of how things become much more understandable:

- One week in the life of an average person = 9 DiBs, assuming an 81-year life.
- $50,000 income compared to $1 B (billion) would be about 2 DiBs.
- $535 million in government grants to the now-bankrupt company Solyndra, which made solar panels. Some in Congress cited this as a scandalous example of government waste. Compared to the total US spending in 2012—$3.5 trillion— this represents about 6 DiBs.

I am not cherry picking an isolated, extreme example. Earlier I was reading an accurate and well-written article in *Time* magazine, but in discussing FDR's New Deal, it said, "The Federal Government that Hoover presided over was stunningly limited in scope. Its entire budget was—fiscal conservatives, read it and weep—under $4 billion."[23] The author—putting on my professor hat—wrote a solid "A" article but does not get a high grade for NBI. There are easy ways to explain the budget in 1930 compared to today. The best probably is as a percent of the whole economy (usually measured as gross domestic product or GDP). Here are the actual figures (all in billions, B):

Year	Federal Budget	Total GDP	Budget as percent of GDP
1930	$4 B	$94 B	5%
2012	$3,700 B	$15,700 B	24%

The above is a much more accurate representation. The point for our NBI crusade is to understand numbers, especially dollar values, in context, or we're likely to be confused. In the article, the author had the opportunity to make a very important point, that the scope of the US government as measured by the budget of the federal government has grown a lot (by about four times) since 1930. He failed to make this point effectively.

Most people can't even conceive of $4 billion. Those who are more facile with figures may have a sense of how big (or small) $4 billion is but can't do the conversion to today's dollars. What's the harm in this? Time is read by millions of people, including many national and international leaders. If writers who are read by hundreds of millions of people would pay a bit more attention to NBI, many aspects of American society would be improved. And, yes, my job as a college professor would be a little easier.

---

23   Adam Cohen, "The First 100 Days," *Time*, July 6, 2009, p. 33.

Another game that politicians, television broadcasters, and department stores play with percentages is not distinguishing between percentages and percentage points. Here's a simple example: Let's say the rate of inflation in 1994 was 5%. What does this mean? Average goods that cost $500 on January 1, 1994, would cost $525 on December 31, 1994. That's simple enough if it's presented that way, so long as people agree we are talking about the annual inflation rate.

But what about those pesky critters, percentage points? They are needed because of possible confusion. Returning to our example, what if the rate of inflation went from 5% to 10%? How much did it increase? Most people's initial reaction would be to say it increased by 5%, but is that accurate? A 5% increase from 5% would produce a new rate of 5.25%— much, much less than 10%. To clarify things, we should talk about percentage points. In this example, a 5 percentage point increase to our 5% inflation rate would produce the 10% rate.

 Look carefully. A 5 percentage point increase in the inflation rate from 5% to 10% is an increase of 100%!

As luck would have it, just as I was writing this sentence, I heard a Republican congressman being interviewed. He stated—with a level of concern and solemnity only members of the US Congress can muster—that since President Obama took office, the unemployment rate has increased by 33%. That sounds really scary and for many people probably creates the image of breadlines and people carrying "will work for food" signs like those seen in the Great Depression of the 1930s when the real unemployment exceeded 30%. I believe this congressman was seeking political shock value by exaggerating the problem he was trying to blame on the Democrats.

Here are actual figures taken from the US government's Bureau of Labor Statistics:

Dec. 2008 unemployment rate: 7.1%
July 2009 unemployment rate: 9.7%
Increase from Dec. to July: 2.6 percentage points
Increase from Dec. to July: 37%

You can see how bouncing back and forth between percentages and percentage points can be extremely confusing, especially for those who aren't comfortable with figures. NBI insists on a crystal-clear distinction. Often this confusion is unintentional when nerdy college professor types like me assume too much knowledge on the part of their audience.

Below is another example of the confusion that can be created by not distinguishing between percent and percentage points.

Fareed Zakaria's *GPS* on CNN reported that extreme poverty in Venezuela was down 70%.

I watch Dr. Zakaria often, enjoy his commentaries, and usually agree with him. Zakaria had some very insightful analyses about what happened to Venezuela under its socialist president Hugo Chavez, who was in power from 1999 until his death in March of 2013. However, in this discussion Zakaria sensationalized and did not clearly explain Chavez's success in reducing Venezuela's poverty rate. He stated that Chavez had reduced the poverty rate by 50% and the extreme poverty rate by 70% since 2004.[24] He should have clearly explained the difference between percent and percentage points and shown actual poverty rates.

For example, it is easy to assume (incorrectly) that extreme poverty went from 77% to 7%. The graph below shows Chavez's success. There

24 Zakaria, Fareed. "What's in Store for Venezuela?" GPS. CNN. 13 Jan. 2013. Television. 1:00 p.m. ET

had been a lot of progress; the extreme poverty rate went down from 24% to 7%, and the poverty rate went down from 53% to 27%.[25] It would not have been difficult to explain it this way, but it might have made it less likely to grab viewers' attention.

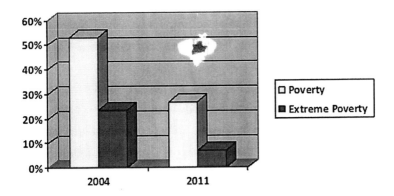

Here's an example from a completely different area. On the local weather forecast, the staff meteorologist, using the latest Doppler-pinpoint-n-dimensional-see-it-before-it-happens radar announces that tonight we will have west winds of about 10 miles per hour. I have done an informal unscientific study and found that about half of Americans think "west winds" come *from* the west and half think they go *to* the west. This is not a minor technical distinction; the last time I looked at a map, east and west were opposites! Why is this confusion allowed to occur? Because people don't demand NBI. To protect myself from rain on all my parades stemming from the American Meteorological Association's crack cloud-seeding unit, I admit that some local weather forecasts do use weather maps with arrows to show wind directions and some even say that "winds are from the west at 10 miles per hour."

---

25   Weisbrot, Mark, and Jake Johnston. *Venezuela's Economic Recovery: Is It Sustainable?* Center for Economic and Policy Research, Sept. 2012. Web. 14 Jan. 2013.

I like statistics. I think colleges should teach more statistics and less calculus, at least for students not majoring in science or engineering. So let's go over a few basics. When I asked my colleagues—Dr. Eric Corty (professor of psychology and author of two great introductory texts on statistics[26]) and Dr. Mike Rutter (associate professor of statistics)—to look over this section, I was afraid they would cry. They did not (at least that I could see), and this section is better for their advice.

While statistics can be used to confuse and distort, NBI is more likely to be improved by understanding them. There is an old saying used most often by people who fear and do not understand statistics: "There are three kinds of lies: lies, damn lies, and statistics."[27]

 Lies, damn lies, and statistics—cute, but it's not that simple.

Dr. Corty's text states that statistics are "techniques used to summarize data in order to answer questions." [28] That not-so-simple assertion is a good jumping off point for our brief visit to a few ideas from statistics. One of the major foci of introductory statistics is measures of central tendency. There are practical reasons for this. Human beings need ways to cope with and to understand massive amounts of information. When we lived in caves, communicated only in an oral language, and interacted mostly with an extended family,

---

26 Eric Corty, *Using and Interpreting Statistics*, Mosby/Elsevier (2007). and Eric Corty, *Using and Interpreting Statistics,* 2nd ed., Worth Publishers (2014).

27 There is uncertainty who originated this phrase but it usually is attributed to Benjamin Disraeli, Conservative Party prime minister of the United Kingdom (Britain) from 1874 to 1880.

28 Eric Corty, *Using and Interpreting Statistics*, 2nd ed., Worth Publishers (2014). I have benefitted from Dr. Corty's explanatory style. His books are excellent for those who want a deeper understanding of statistics but who think calculus should be limited to something the dental hygienist scrapes off your teeth. Quotation from p. 1.

tribe, or clan, people had a much smaller volume of information. Most of it was pretty simple, e.g., be careful not to be eaten by that saber-toothed tiger.

Today, virtually everyone is faced with a confusing mass of information that comes at us constantly from all directions. Don't be scared away by the name; "measures of central tendency" are like a very funny ballet written 350 years ago by French dramatist Molière, whose character Monsieur Jourdain proclaims, "By my faith! For more than forty years I have been speaking prose without knowing anything about it, and I am much obliged to you for having taught me that."[29] You might not know it but you have been "speaking" central tendency much of your life.

 I am bilingual: Greek and central tendency.

Let me illustrate with an example I confront many times a year—assigning grades to my students. Most fall semesters I teach a political science class often with about 100 students. If they read the syllabus, those students will know exactly how they will be graded, such as what percentage the final exam counts, penalties for skipping class, and so forth. At the end of the semester, I have to give a grade to each student. For this example I broke down the earned grades into nine ranges:

55-59%	80-84%
60-64%	85-89%
65-69%	90-94%
70-74%	95-99%
75-79%	

---

29 The Bourgeois Gentleman (Le Bourgeois gentilhomme) is a five-act comédie-ballet—a ballet interrupted by spoken dialogue—by Molière, first presented on October 14, 1670. Available online athttp://www.gutenberg.org/catalog/world/readfile?fk_files=3275173

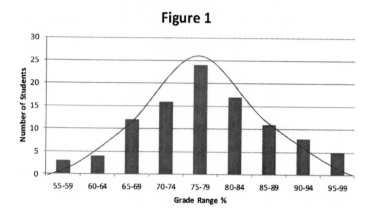

Figure 1

Let's assume I have a class of exactly 100 (so 100% will equal number of students) in Fall 2013. To make it easy, assume further this is a fairly typical class and I am able to assign grades to all the students. Figure 1 shows the number and percent who fell within each possible grade range. I'll use this to introduce a few basic ideas about statistics, specifically central tendency, and, in the next chapter, sampling.

This is a simple, straightforward example. Each one of the nine grade ranges is listed on the bottom of the chart. The bars represent the number of students in each grade range. Recall that there are 100 students, so each is 1% of the total. The curve of the data is nearly symmetrical with most students in the middle and the number of students declining as we move to the extremes, such as grades in the 95-99 percent range or those in the 55-59% range. This is what statisticians call a normal distribution, which is shown by the bell-shaped line. Even in this uncomplicated example—only 100 students and the simplest, most predictable distribution—we still would like a way to summarize the grades. I need something to tell the kids when they e-mail me to complain about their grades and I face that unpleasant moment for a professor: Students who received a "C" deserved a "D" and are complaining because they did not get a "B."

OK, Gamble, stop feeling sorry for yourself. You know you love your job.

How might we go about clearly describing the 100 values (grades) in Figure 1? Measures of central tendency of course! The most common such measure is called the average or more accurately the mean.

- You calculate the average (or mean) by adding all the values and dividing by the total number (here, 100).

This calculation produces a value of about 78, which translates to a C+ on my grading scale. Thus we can say the average final grade given in my class was a 78%%, or a C+. That's important information, and you can bet students are interested both in their own grades and how they compare with others in the class.[30]

The mean or average is not the only measure of central tendency. Two others commonly used are the median and mode. They are even easier to explain.

- The median is the middle score. If all scores (my students' grades in this example) are ranked from worst to best, the median is the middle value.

Look at Figure 1, and you can guess that the median is in the middle grade range 75-79. In fact, when analyzing the raw scores, I find the median to be 78, which is the same as the mean score. The final measure of central tendency we'll talk about is the mode, the simplest of all.

---

30 I direct the honors program at my college of Penn State and, in that capacity, deal with many great students. My advice to them is don't worry about grades, work hard, and let grades take care of themselves. Only one honors student has followed my advice completely. He/she would not want me to mention her/his name, but my hat is off to her/him. Note the good job of not revealing the gender of the person and that, unlike most writers, I do not always put the male pronoun first.

- The mode is the score (grade) that occurs most often.

Here, the mode also is 78, because it was the score given to the greatest number of students. I know what you're thinking—"I hate statistics, and this damn professor is telling me about three different measures, each of which produces the same result. Why not limit it to the average so I can don my NBI T-shirt and begin the fight?" Good point, but remember my first example is an almost-perfect bell curve—in statistician's parlance, a normal distribution. It is a bit like driving on the interstate on a cloudless day with almost no traffic. The real world often is much different, more like a crowded, curvy road on a windy, snowy day. Information (data) usually is not so regular.

Figure 2

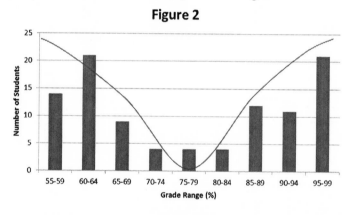

Figure 2 represents a stunningly different class. Can you imagine me trying to teach the "kids" in this class? Fully one-third are "A" students and another third are D and F students. There is an old saying that you have to teach to the middle. In the case of Figure 1, I've got a large middle to teach to (not to be confused with teaching with a large middle that I try to avoid by exercising about 600 miles a year). A group like Figure 2 is enough to make an old professor pull out the little hair he has left. If I tried to teach the Figure 2 group, I probably could not do a very good job. If I aimed at the middle, I'd bore the big clump of A students and go too fast for the equally large group of D and F students.

The mean, median, and mode together give you a clearer view.

I think I have found a way to entice you to follow me through one last concept before I move on to easier, more intuitive material. Statisticians seek ways to describe different kinds of distributions, such as the grades my students get. The mean, median, and mode helped us to understand this. But we also must think about deviation. Relax—this is not what you might be imagining. Deviation is how far the average student score is away from the average (or mean). For a reason I will not explain in depth, statisticians often calculate the standard deviation, a statistic that shows how widely dispersed scores are. For example, if all of my students got a 70%, the standard deviation would be zero!

Look at Figures 1 and 2. Figure 1 has the most grades near the middle range of 75-79%. There is no deviation from the mean for those students who got a 78% because they are exactly at the average. If you include students that got grades within the middle three ranges (in total from 70-84%), you get more than half of all the students.[31] The standard deviation for Figure 1 is about 9 percentage points. It is clear from looking at either figure that some deviation is above the mean (average), and of course some is below. When you go from one standard deviation about the mean to one below, you include about two-thirds of the cases (about 68 students). Look at the table below: In Class #1 you only have to use scores from 69% to 87% to get two-thirds of students. Now look at Class #2. You see the scores are spread out much more, making the standard deviation much greater. In fact, we would have to include all the grades from 63% to 93% (F through A) to get about the same two-thirds. The standard deviation shows us how widely scattered the scores are.

---

31   In a perfect bell curve, 68% of the data points fall in this range.

Here's a summary of what we've learned about these two classes:

Measure of Central Tendency	Class #1	Class #2
Mean grade	78 (C+)	77 (C+)
Mode grade	78 (C+)	62 (F)
Median grade	78 (C+)	77 (C+)
2 standard deviations 68% of grades)	69% to 87% (D to B)	63% to 93% (F to A)

It's been 50 years since I first learned about standard deviation. The concept did not come easily, and it often does not come easily to my students. Think about this very simple illustration. Assume we want to calculate the average weight of two very small groups of people—three per group.

	Group #1	Group #2
Person 1	90 lbs.	167 lbs.
Person 2	170 lbs.	167 lbs.
Person 3	241 lbs.	167 lbs.

You should be thinking that, with only two groups of three people each, you could readily see how different the two groups are. With a pen and paper (or calculator) you could determine that the average weight for each group is the same—167 pounds. Computing the standard deviation gives us a number showing how different these groups are even though the means (averages) are identical. Group #1 has a standard deviation of about 75½ pounds. What about Group #2? The standard deviation is zero pounds. When you have large groups you wish to understand and compare, standard deviation can be a big help.

You don't have to know any more about standard deviations than we've just covered to use the concept as a powerful weapon against bull-laden information. Whenever you hear a political leader, a salesperson or a news anchor talk loosely about the average (mean), here is what you do: Stare intently at them, pause about ten seconds and ask, "What is the standard deviation?" If that does not finish them off, pause exactly two more seconds, and say *sigma*, the Greek letter (σ) often used to denote standard deviation. Trust me, this will work. I've seen silver-tongued used car salesmen reduced to stuttering[32] to the point of incomprehensibility or, more commonly, have to run to the restroom.

Congratulations, you've completed what for most of you is the most tedious portion of this book. But this brief refresher about numbers will pay big dividends (understood both as percentages or percentage points) as you pursue NBI. You don't have to become an expert. There is a comforting irony in the fact the knowledge you've gained here can make you confident in proclaiming to a mayoral candidate or a used car salesperson, "I don't understand how your average was calculated—please explain."

---

32 Apologies to my readers who stutter. I have stuttered for more than 60 years and realize that real stuttering is totally different from a normal speaker who becomes stressed and flustered.

CHAPTER 5

SAMPLING, RANKINGS— OFTEN DECEPTIVE

S ampling might be the most useful part of statistics to advance our goal of NBI in modern American society.

We usually talk about a population, i.e., the whole group defined for a particular purpose. A sample is a smaller number taken from the population.

For example, suppose we want to know what portion of people eat a good diet defined as an adequate amount of healthy food. What population are we talking about? We might mean the entire world (about seven billion people) or just the US (about 330 million people). The population we are talking about can make a huge difference, so we must make clear the group we are discussing. We might mean college students, Pennsylvania residents, US residents or everyone in the world.

 I am a sample of one. What I do, see, and feel does not represent others.

Let's assume we are asking about the diets of Americans. Putting aside the issue of how we can assess the diets and whether people will be honest about how many Buffalo wings they consume per fortnight, we could not possibly ask all 330 million Americans. Almost always a sample is taken with the goal of accurately predicting the entire population from that sample. Statisticians can prove that a random sample of about 2,000 people usually is quite accurate—within a couple of percentage points—of predicting the entire population. It is much easier to ask 2,000 people than 330 million. But what is a random sample? Each member of the population must have an equal chance of being included in the sample. That's a clear goal but damned difficult to achieve.

Those who study sampling and polling often point to a survey done by *The Literary Digest*, a popular American magazine in the first half of the 20th century. The digest conducted a poll to predict the results of the 1936 presidential election between President Franklin Roosevelt (Democrat from New York) and Governor Alf Landon (Republican from Kansas). The Digest's poll predicted an overwhelming win for Governor Landon by about 60% to 40%.[33] The results were almost the reverse with President Roosevelt receiving nearly 60%. Many believe that, when the magazine went out of business a couple of years later, it was because of this fiasco.

---

33   *Literary Digest*, 31 October 1936.

Very large samples can produce terrible results.

How could this have happened? When predictions based on samples do a terrible job, usually it is because they do not accurately represent the population, but why? You can have a sample so small that the chances of representing all important attitudes are almost zero. Or you can have a sample—perhaps even a very large one—that is not representative. That's what occurred with *The Literary Digest* poll. Their sample size was enormous—2.5 million—about 3% of all eligible voters in 1936. How did they get it so wrong?

The cause of this monumental screw-up is clear: Their sample was grossly unrepresentative, not even close to random.[34] The magazine used three sources for its sample: subscribers, names in telephone books, and automobile registration listings. Today such sources might do a pretty good job, but in 1936 all three produced a sample that was much wealthier than the typical American. In 1936 and even today, wealthier Americans are more likely to vote for Republican candidates. So that's the reason for this monumental skew-up [sic].[35]

NBI requires you to be on the lookout for sampling mistakes. Some are unintentional, many are blatant fabrications. Others are technically true but, if you think carefully about them, they have gigantic sampling problems. Consider this brief hypothetical example "inspired" by TV ads that seem to be in my face so often that I feel the urge to use my middle finger when I press the mute button on the remote.

---

34 Squire, Peverill. "Why the 1936 Literary Digest Poll Failed." *The Public Opinion Quarterly* 52.1 (Spring 1988): 125-33. *JSTOR.* Web. 9 Jan. 2013.

35 Skewed data or information is quite distorted from what is expected with a normal distribution. So I am calling this a "skew-up" instead of a screwup. "Sic"—as you should remember—is an abbreviation in Latin for "as such." It is used to show that the preceding word or phrase is written exactly as intended in spite of the fact it may appear to be an error.

Save money and put your trust in the Smallrock Insurance Company (SmaKinCo). The average driver who switched to SmaKinCo from Lizzardco Mutual saved $519 per year on car insurance. The average driver who switched to SmaKinCo from InterStatePrairie (ISP) saved a staggering $910 per year. That's not all, studies show that 95% of SmaKinCo customers rate their auto insurance as good, very good, or excellent.

There are more sampling problems in the above than "like ya knows" in the daily conversation of a college student.[36] Sampling is really important here. The $519 figure might be accurate and based on thousands of customers, but—a huge but—if you call SmaKinCo and ask them how much you can save and they tell you $2 a year, will you switch? In this instance, their sample is skewed—distorted— towards those who were able to save a lot of money and chose to switch. SmaKinCo did not lie, but those who do not think carefully about the wording of the ad might be deceived. I would bet the sample size for those switching from ISP to SmaKinCo (hope you're observing the power of acronyms) is extremely small.

Furthermore, NBI does not like embellishment of already-precise information. In this case, is a "staggering $910" more money than a "piddling $910"? We don't need this kind of "help." I'd like to see the sample used to calculate the 95%. Did they include customers who had accidents and had their rates raised? Did they limit their survey to those who never had to file a claim? Even if the sample were large and random, the exact wording of the choices offered can affect the results.

What if the survey went like this?

---

36 Sorry for what may be perceived as a cheap shot. I spend much of my working life trying to improve the verbal skills of 18-22- year-old kids. The incidence of the utterly meaningless filler "like ya know" is amazing. At the beginning of the 2011 school year, I overheard a conversation between two freshmen. It began "Like ya know, I don't know . . ." It was enough to make me want to study existentialism.

Please select the one that best describes your satisfaction with your SmaKinCo car insurance:

- 0% superb
- 0% excellent
- 6% very good
- 89% good
- 0% poor
- 5% terrible

The 95% does not look nearly as positive when viewed in this light. Some distortion like this can be well intentioned.

An old friend of mine owns two car dealerships in Erie. When I take my car in for service, they give me a survey about my experience. It has a red stamp saying, "If you cannot give us the highest possible ratings, please phone us at XXX-XXXX immediately so we can correct any problems." This procedure might improve their service and be effective for advertising, but it will not win any NBI awards.

Here is another aspect of the sampling issue: There is a popular expression that has recently been rediscovered—"You are entitled to your own opinion, but not to your own facts."[37] Lawrence O'Donnell, an MSNBC commentator, uses the expression to advertise his television show. I usually agree with Mr. O'Donnell and commend the higher-than-normal information standards he sets. That said, the idea that we are not entitled to our own facts does not go nearly far enough. There are cases where leaders, entertainers, college students, professors, and others make statements that simply are wrong. They make up facts; sometimes it is clear what they are doing. Some of these statements are trivial, some silly, and anyone with half a brain will dismiss them.

---

37 Quote attributed to Senator Daniel Patrick Moynihan. US Congress. "Congressional Record," Volume 151, Part 8. 19 May, 2005 to 6 June, 2005. Pg. 10,820.

The principal danger may be the numbing of our senses so much that we cannot easily switch to demanding NBI standards when it becomes essential. But let's put aside—at least for now—clearly inaccurate "facts" such as 2012 vice presidential candidate Paul Ryan saying he had run a marathon in "two hours and fifty something [minutes]."[38] The average marathon time for men is around four hours and twenty-seven minutes; Paul Ryan's time was just over four hours; the world record is just under two hours and four minutes.[39] Remember a central theme of this book is that getting facts correct is just the first step.

 Find accurate facts, but then put them into context.

Rankings: A Love Affair America Should Control

There is an understandable appeal to rankings. By rankings, I mean attempts to put an order to things, e.g., from best to worst. There are times when rankings can be valuable. Let's assume we have a sports league with these characteristics:

- 10 teams
- each team plays every other team 10 times in the season
- ties are not permitted under the rules of this game

Given these conditions, the win/loss records of the teams would be a good indicator of the quality of the teams. If the Meadville Rabid Dogs[40] has 90 wins and no losses, it probably deserves to be #1, especially since no other team could have more than 80 wins.

---

38   Ryan, Paul. "Paul Ryan Phone Interview on the Hugh Hewitt Show." Interview by Hugh Hewitt. *Townhall Radio*. 22 Aug. 2012. Web. 9 Jan. 2013.

39   "Makau stuns with 2:03:38 Marathon World record in Berlin!" International Association of Athletics Federation. 25 September, 2011.

40   See Willi Strong, in Chapter 8.

Rankings as clear as those earned by the Rabid Dogs are rare. Let's continue with the sports analogy using the same 10 teams, but make these changes:

- have two divisions (Eastern and Western), five teams each
- each team plays 15 games against each opponent in its division and five against each team in the other division.

We could still rank all 10 teams by overall win/loss record, but this might be much less useful for ranking. Anyone with even a modicum of interest in sports has heard arguments like this: "Maybe the Mad Dogs have the best record at 90% wins, but their division [or league or conference] was much easier." I am not going to delve more deeply into sports. My passion in this book is information, how it is used and abused, not sports.[41]

We Americans are bombarded with rankings. Why such an attraction? I see three principal reasons:

- Rankings are a simple and appealing way to navigate through the mass of information in an age named for information.
- Americans often are brought up to be competitive. This results in a desire not only to be a winner but to observe and try to understand winners and winning.
- The mass media love rankings. They are sensational, make for easy headlines, and attract more viewers/readers.

What's wrong with all of this? A competitive, results-oriented individualistic society like America should pay attention to rankings as part of our quest to make ourselves better and to recognize achievement.

---

41   Except of course my passion for the Rabid Dogs, a fictious team from my real hometown.

But hold on a minute—all rankings are not created equal. Most are not nearly as valid as the first sports example above, 10 teams each of which plays the other nine teams 10 times. At the other end of the continuum are rankings that may be fun, get headlines in the newspaper, but should not be taken seriously except for their entertainment value.

A somewhat sensitive example is Barbara Walters, a path-breaking television journalist, interviewer, and recently retired talk show host. Ms. Walters overcame huge and grossly unfair barriers to land a job on *The Today Show* and later to co-host *ABC Evening News*. She has gotten interviews with some of the most important people in the world and can be fearless in her questioning. However, since 1993, Ms. Walters has hosted a show once a year called *Barbara Walters' 10 Most Fascinating People*.[42] In 2012 she explained the criteria she used to make her choices: "people who have been 'very much in the news' and 'no criminals.' "[43] In 2012 she named David Petraeus[44] #1, asserting, "This is about military honor, colliding with sex and lies in the digital age."[45]

Why am I dissatisfied with Ms. Walters? I watch some of her shows. The selections are Ms. Walters's judgments about who is most fascinating. She has every right to her choices. However, the show, articles, and her choices receive billing that seem like a scientifically conducted survey on frequency of major diseases in the US. The lesson is we must look carefully at rankings before getting carried away. It usually is far easier to criticize than to improve, so here is my suggestion for Ms. Walters:

"Barbara Walters, who, over the last third of a century has interviewed some of the most important people in the world, will introduce you to the 10 people she has judged to be the most fascinating in 2014."

---

42   http://www.people.com/people/article/0,,20656001,00.html
43   http://www.nypost.com/p/pagesix/barbara_walters_most_fascinating_ymf9qlVWzYUOmZtizBfJHI
44   A four-star general and CIA Director. Petraeus resigned from his CIA position citing an extramarital affair.
45   http://www.usatoday.com/story/life/people/2012/12/13/barbara-walters-unveils-most-fascinating-person-2012/1766045/

Ms. Walters's shows can be really interesting, but I hope most of my readers will understand these are not rankings in a meaningful sense. Rather they show Ms. Walters's opinions, and fortunately she uses the descriptor "fascinating" rather than "important" or "influential." When you run across rankings like Ms. Walters's, you should put them into context by considering they are one person's opinion about something very subjective—who is "fascinating." Part of the context should be that Ms. Walters, over the last 50 years, has met face to face and interviewed many extremely important people.

I am confident you can put examples like those given above in their proper place—entertainment if you want it, but of little additional value. There are many other examples where the rankings seem rigorous and scientific. Below I have created a hypothetical ranking of hypothetical automobiles, simplified but illustrating important points about the scrutiny you should give to all rankings.

Rankings of 2014 Small Sport Utility Vehicles (SUVs)
Overall Score (100 = maximum)

1. Delta Mountain Climber 2.5*i*	92
2. Roosevelt CBQT 3.0 cid	91
3. Ledviev Off-Roader Hybrid	86
4. Dakota Explorer 3.3*i*	80
5. Deutsch-max Autobahn 2.0 TDI	80
6. Rising Sun Go-All 3.0*i* 5c	72
7. Cape Cod Conqueror S 2.2	60
8. Lyon tout le monde 1.8*i*	59
9. Brasilia ilimitado AFV	51
10. Maritime Horizons 2.0T	49

Many ratings you see, not just those for automobiles, are no better than the above. And they often "inspire" headlines like "2013 Delta Mountain Climber 2.5i Rated Best in Class."

What's wrong with this? There are so many deficiencies I hardly know where to start.

1. Who did the ratings? How knowledgeable and objective were they?
2. Did the car companies provide free cars for the tests?
3. Who defined the class—small SUV? Can manufacturers redefine a class so they win?
4. What goes into the ratings, and how are they weighted? For example, safety, reliability, and fuel mileage all are important. Are they weighted equally?
5. Is price taken into account? What if the Roosevelt 3.2 CBQT diesel (score 91) costs $31,500 and the Delta Mountain Climber 2.5 l (score 92) costs $39,900?
6. In the above illustration and in many real-world examples, ranking can cause a major misreading of the information. Scores can be virtually identical, in which case ranking introduces false precision. Does the Dakota Explorer 3.3 I (score 80) really deserve a higher rating than the Deutsch-max Autobahn 2.0 TDI (also a score of 80). It's better to declare a tie rather than letting alphabetical order determine the winner.

Part of my job as a professor is advising undergraduates about attending law school. People pay enormous attention to the *U.S. News* Best Law Schools issue.[46] This source does a pretty good job of balancing many factors and indicating clearly what information is used. The *U.S. News* rankings have ties, real ties. If you have a virtual tie for #1 ranking among three schools, you should rank all #1, on the same line at the top.

---

46 http://grad-schools.usnews.rankingsandreviews.com/best-graduate-schools/top-law-schools/law-rankings

Far too few people are willing to confront the limitations and be diligent in assessing ranking systems. With regard to law schools and higher education generally, lack of scrutiny is especially blatant when deans and college presidents are critical of the *U.S. News* rankings when their colleges' rankings decline and loudly and instantly sing the praises of the same *U.S. News* system when the results are positive.

 You must not brag about your ranking one year and criticize the entire ranking process the next.

I could write much more about rankings but hope this is enough to convince you to be suspicious and to ask questions. Often entertainment is the only value of rankings.

FILTERING OUT THE BULL

People need to learn how to protect themselves or at least get an early warning of a number of ways in which bull-laden information can pierce their intellectual armor and make them behave in stupid ways. The strategies that follow can be like a flu shot that provides the human body with an automatic system of resistance when certain viruses invade it. In this instance, we need ways to protect against being taken over and forced to act irrationally.

Rx3 # 5 On Shakespeare's Language and S.H.It

I love the English language (Shakespeare's language as I often call it) and on a good writing day I have become proficient in its use. I've spent thousands of hours talking to college students, often testing how English can be used more effectively. I believe English is a medium capable of explaining very complex things, but it can be tough. This task of explanation becomes even harder if we are afraid of sounds and are obsessed with political correctness. The goal of No-Bull Information becomes even more difficult to achieve if we have to worry about similarities in sounds of words. An example of sensitivity about word usage is whether to use male pronouns, the tradition in English. Some alternate between male and female pronouns. More common is using both the female and male pronouns with a slash in between, e.g., he/she and him/her. I often use the slash approach but I alphabetize the pronouns, e.g., he/she and her/him. Is all of this worth the effort?[47] I make a joke in my classes by using the super politically correct, cover-all-the-bases acronym, "S.H.It" that means (you've guessed it) "she", "he" or "it." My students tell me S.H.It has another meaning, but I think they are pulling my chain.

In order to be proficient in NBI, you must learn to think longer term and more analytically. You need to avoid one type of prejudice that is an inevitable part of being human: assuming that your individual life experiences are similar to those of others. This is part of the sampling problem covered in Chapter 5. Everybody has been bombarded by "traditional wisdom" from schoolyard friends to our grandparents. Some information we received was accurate, some harmless, some pretty intelligent, some dead wrong and almost all oversimplified. NBI requires that we look beyond these prejudices as part of thinking more

---

47 Two arguments can be made. Use of the male pronoun in all situations where there is a choice, e.g., always referring to a US president as "him," can subtly—or not so subtly—create the impression in millions of people that the president must be male. Others have argued that everyone knows that "him" does not mean it cannot be a woman. Further, if you are attempting the difficult task of changing behavior, do you want to spend your time and energy encouraging people to watch their pronouns? Is it possible that a new pattern in pronoun use eventually will change attitudes?

critically. I don't want to take all the fun out of life, but it is necessary to discipline yourself to step out of your experiential shell and realize that even what your beloved aunt told you might not have been accurate. Once you see beyond the box, you can behave like a chess master or football quarterback who sees and uses dozens of options and thinks many steps ahead.

I don't want to ruin fond memories. It is possible to retain simple, beautiful memories and use them as a pathway to analytic thinking. There are many elements to NBI-friendly thinking. We need to anticipate unintended consequences. Human beings often view the world in too narrow, shortsighted a way. I suspect this has its roots in our biological origins where short term meant life or death. If we did not get the short term right, there was no long term. If we made it to long term, that long term was much shorter than today's. NBI requires us to think more analytically and longer term.

 That box represents who I am and where I came from. Use it as a sanctuary from which to think creatively and see longer term.

We should modify that overused expression "think outside the box." That famous box provides the structure people need to navigate through life. It is built from memories from our earliest years. People need the security of the box, but it should be transparent so we can see through and beyond it rather than being confined by it. This is the surest route to the analytical thinking so essential to using NBI. Let me discuss four broad ways to see through and beyond the box and to create the right frame of mind for analytical thinking. To continue the metaphor, we need a sturdy, resilient box in which to live, a box that protects us but through which we can see clearly at great distances and over our entire lives.

1. Unintended consequences

Most governmental actions and business decisions are made with specific goals in mind. Even if programs succeed, they often have huge unintended consequences. I shall discuss examples. The first is the interstate highway system in the US, the brainchild of President Dwight D. Eisenhower. One of the principal reasons for the system was military—to move tanks and troops around easily from one part of the country to another, especially in the case of a nuclear attack on a major city.[48] It also may have something to do with the fact Eisenhower loved cars and was a backyard mechanic.[49] Although it took decades and hundreds of billions of dollars to complete, we now have a network of interstate highways.

The second example is US actions during World War II, a time of unimaginable sadness, punctuated by occasional moments of joy and an economy working at peak capacity, due to the need for products and services brought on by the war. Most knowledge of Americans is focused on winning the war. Public awareness 70 years later of the Holocaust, D-Day, General Eisenhower, and the atomic bombs dropped on Japan remains high. Often forgotten is what we did on the home front to win the war. One small cog in our giant war machine was wage and price controls. Wartime needs for everything from rubber, to butter, to stockings, to cigarettes meant that the free market had to be controlled. We could not let supply and demand set the price of butter, or only rich people would have been able to afford it. We instituted rationing for many items through the use of coupon books. Because more than 16 million Americans served in the armed forces,[50]

48 United States. The White House. Office of the Press Secretary to the President. *Message to the Congress Regarding Highways.* By Dwight D. Eisenhower. Ed. James C. Hagerty. Feb. 22, 1955. *Archives.gov.* Dwight D. Eisenhower Presidential Library and Museum. Web. 30 Jan. 2013.
49 Korda, Michael. IKE: *An American Hero.* NY: Harper Perennial, 2008. Print.
50 http://www.wwiimemorial.com/

there was a shortage of workers on the home front, requiring wage and price controls.

Our industrial production was astounding: US industry produced nearly two-thirds of all Allied equipment during the war, and the US doubled its industrial output from 1941-45; at the end of the war, the US was producing more than half of the world's industrial goods.[51] However, many industries faced with labor shortages and wage controls during the war needed to find a way to attract good workers. One way was to offer health insurance—not controlled like wages—to their workers.[52] This worked for a while but set the US on a path (allocation of a value) followed by few other countries.

Seventy years later we still try to follow this model, but it has become grossly inefficient; we spend more on healthcare than any other country (in actual dollars and as a percent of GDP)[53] and do not get the best results. Although wage and price controls enabled the US to better manage its resources, certainly contributing to the Allied victory in World War II, those controls also led to a system in which employers used healthcare benefits to attract workers, a model that continued even after the war ended, instead of the government offering healthcare the way most other countries do.

 Hard to believe, but winning World War II is a major cause of the healthcare financing crisis of today.

Returning to the example of the interstate highway system, we spent so much public money on the highway system—in essence a

---

51 http://www.pbs.org/thewar/at_home_war_production.htm

52 For more information about the history of employer-based healthcare, see this excellent article: Alex Blumberg and Adam Davidson, *Accidents of History Created the U.S. Health System*, NPR accessed online (2009).

53 For these statistics and many more about the cost of healthcare in the United States relative to other developed countries see Jason Kane, *Health Costs: How the U.S. Compares With Other Countries*, PBS—accessed online (2012).

massive subsidy to the trucking industry and to passenger cars—that passenger rail service in the US has almost disappeared. Today, you can get reasonably good passenger service in a few places such as the Washington to Boston corridor but little elsewhere.

Many scholars believe that the interstate highway system made it easier for wealthier people—who owned more cars—to leave the interior of large cities. Since highways made automobile travel much faster, wealthy people no longer had to live in close proximity to their place of work and could commute from the suburbs. Although this trend started before highways were built, it accelerated once the highway system was completed.

This exacerbated the concentration of poor people in urban areas while those with higher incomes fled to the suburbs. This also had an unintended consequence on the education system. Since major funding for schools comes from property taxes—the revenues of which depend on property values—concentrated poverty meant that inner-city schools became underfunded, which also led to a "brain drain" from these areas as the most qualified teachers sought better employment elsewhere. The economic and social decay in many large US cities was an unfortunate, unintended consequence of the interstate highway system.[54]

In many Western European countries, such as Britain, governments assumed the primary responsibility for providing universal healthcare to citizens. This led to more efficient systems of healthcare administration. In the US, no such system was created. The system that was put into place during the war—one in which the private employers were responsible for providing healthcare—continued after the war ended, an unintended consequence of wage and price controls.

---

54 Deakin, Elizabeth. *The Social Impacts of the Interstate Highway System: What Are the Repercussions?* Paper No 799. Berkeley: University of California Transportation Center, 2006. Print.

That system worked well for a while, as unemployment remained low immediately following the war. But over time this system became less reliable for the average citizen as employment became increasingly uncertain in rougher economic times. And since the US government wasn't as involved as other countries in providing healthcare, it was also less involved in reducing and managing the rising costs. To this day, Americans are affected by the unintended consequences of the employer insurance program that started during World War II as a result of wage and price controls. Americans receive lower quality healthcare and pay more for it than people in many other developed countries.

Everything has consequences, some of which must be unintended! If we worry too much about unintended consequences, we will be frozen into inaction. Nothing would ever change. We'd still be a British colony with only land-owning white males allowed to vote. It is a matter of balance. Force yourself to consider what unintended consequences might ensue from specific actions, e.g., proposals from politicians running for office.

In the example of the interstate highway system, I am not saying we should have refused to build new highways. What if there had been a tax on gasoline of 10% (instead of an amount that fails to keep up with inflation) to be used to assure we had modern, high-speed intercity rail lines? See the less obvious; look through the box. Practice makes this easier. More people should do it.

2. Overly simple notions of cause and effect

People crave certainty and predictability to cope with life. While that may be necessary for society to function, it can also create a huge need in people to snatch simplicity and order from the jaws of complexity. Up to a point, that's fine. Achieving a balance is vital for analytical thinking. One particularly important aspect is cause and effect.

Determining cause and effect relationships is complicated by two problems. The first problem is that of the "missing variable" or "third variable." You can calculate the relationship between two things, e.g., years in school and income, and this is called correlation. However, even if you discover a strong association between two things, e.g., increased sales of air conditioning units and increased cases of heat stroke, it does not prove a cause/effect relationship. AC units do not cause heat stroke; there is a third variable, i.e., increased heat in the summer, that links the other two variables. The real cause and effect relationship probably has more to do with increased heat leading to an increase in both air conditioner sales and cases of heat stroke. Looking for "third variables" in correlational relationships will help protect you from dubious cause/effect assumptions.

A second problem in determining cause and effect relationships is the problem of "directionality." Even if you determine that a cause and effect relationship exists between two things, it may be difficult to determine the direction of the cause. For example, let's imagine that we found a relationship between gun sales and violent crime. Does an increase in gun sales lead to more violent crime because more guns are available to commit crimes? Or does an increase in violent crime lead to an increase in gun sales as people seek to protect themselves from crime? Furthermore, does a decrease in gun sales lead to a decrease in violent crime by making guns less available, or does a decrease in violent crime make people feel safer and lead to decreased gun sales?

 Be extremely careful before assuming cause and effect.

Cause and effect is one of the first things a human being learns. A baby cries and its mother (or father) feeds S.H.It.[55] Both the baby

---

55   This book requires you to remember stuff mentioned previously—S.H.It is an acronym for "She He or It."

and the feeder quickly see a cause/effect relationship. Hunger creates an unpleasant feeling that produces the crying. The crying is interpreted as a sign of hunger that is dealt with by feeding after which the crying subsides. What could be simpler? I'm not a developmental psychologist, but I wonder if we oversimplify even this most basic human action. Babies cry immediately after birth often in connection with starting to breathe. But is crying an inborn response to hunger, or is it learned or taught, or both?

Here's the central point about cause and effect. We see many examples where it appears to be absolutely clear. You stub your toe on a chair leg, it hurts like hell and turns black and blue. That cause/effect is not very complicated. The toe was forced to bend in a way it was not designed to bend; perhaps the inner workings of the toe were damaged. Your body instantly warned you with pain, perhaps excruciating pain. We're supposed to learn from this and that's fine for toe health. But it is not good for NBI if the bruised toe syndrome (BTS) causes us to accept cause/effect assumptions in other areas where they are much less certain.

The mass media often help to create oversimplified notions of cause and effect. Literally[56] as I write this, CNN is reporting on a study in a top medical journal that concluded that men over 40 who have sex more often have fewer heart attacks. The newsreaders have fun with the story and that's fine. But—even with sex—we have to question cause and effect. Does more frequent sex protect against heart attacks, or is it more complicated than that? If a man (the study dealt only with men) is in extremely poor health anyway, he probably is low on a sexual activity scale. Could it be that men who exercise, eat a proper diet, and are not overweight have sex more often? What is the real cause?

---

56   I use "literally" correctly in this case. It was reported on CNN as I wrote.

There is a huge difference between association and causation. If we look at SAT scores of black, white, and yellow Americans[57] we find that the average scores of Asians are highest, followed by whites, with blacks coming in last. No one with half a brain and one eye open believes "blackness" causes lower SAT scores. This is just one example of how we have to be careful with cause and effect.

The dog lovers among my readers are angry that it has been many pages since a reference to my dog, Belle. Belle was quite a clean dog, but she did not like to be bathed. However, like most dogs, she loved to please human beings, especially those who cared for her. Thus it is easy to draw an incorrect conclusion about cause/effect. Here is the sequence:

- Belle is given a bath.
- The bath ends.
- Belle appears very happy.
- Therefore: Belle likes baths.

The above "dog logic" fails in a couple ways. If you watched Belle during the bath, you would have seen she did not like it. Two major factors distort the normal cause/effect relation. First, Belle really wanted to please people. Therefore, she might appear to be happy because she sensed the bath pleases the bath-giver. Second, Belle appeared happiest at the end—why? She sensed the joy in the bath-giver and she was glad to get the damn thing over with!

Matters dealing with people's health are especially prone to cause/effect confusion. People often recover because our bodies are designed to repair themselves. There is a powerful human need to see cause/effect

---

57   Sorry, folks, I could not resist. I submit that "white," "black," and "yellow" are about equally inaccurate. Very few human beings are even close to the "pure" versions of those colors on a color wheel. There are times when I think we should revert to "Caucasoid" "Mongoloid," and "Negroid," the anthropologically correct names for the three principal races that occupy planet earth.

relationships in everything. If my sprained ankle quickly gets better overnight when there is a full moon, did the latter cause the former? In the Information Age, I could go on TV (or the Internet) and proclaim my miracle cure. It's a dangerous combination: health, confusion over cause and effect, and a small sample (one!) all in the Internet age.

The lesson: Analytical thinking requires careful attention to cause and effect. They seldom are as simple as they seem. Cause and effect relationships do exist even when dealing with complex critters like humans. However, there are many examples where yesterday's effect may become tomorrow's cause. People are not as simple as experiments in a test tube.

3. Cost/benefit analysis

Since you've already gotten this far in this book, I'll risk throwing in a bit of economics. Seriously, some of my best friends are economists and, even though economics is called the dismal science, it has a lot to teach us.

Much of the information we are given should be run through a cost/benefit calculator. The TV advertisement that lists the cost of a number of items that can be charged on your MasterCard then proclaims certain things are priceless makes an excellent point. There are things—like stone-skipping and Belle's enthusiasm for licking the chocolate pudding bowl—that really are priceless. But much of the information bombarding us could do with a healthy dose of cost/benefit analysis.

One of the most common examples is income tax deductibility. This technique is used often and by both political parties. Republicans recently advocated a healthcare savings account where people could exempt a portion of their income from taxes in order to save money for healthcare costs. Putting aside whether that is a good idea, you must consider the revenue lost because taxes are not collected. Maybe such programs are good even with the tax deductibility, but that fact must not be ignored. Most charities in the US would have trouble existing were it not for the tax deductibility of the contributions they receive. But if people really believe in the charity, why do they need a tax deduction to motivate them to contribute?

 If a politician offers a tax cut or tax credit, demand to know how much it costs and how S.H.It will pay for it.

Cost/benefit analysis can be difficult and controversial. The US defense budget for 2013 was approximately $822 billion. How could you do a cost/benefit analysis on this? Accurately measuring the value of effectively protecting the nation is extremely difficult.

If we are not attacked by a terrorist or foreign power for a year, does this mean we are getting good benefit for the billions spent? Should we give the Pentagon everything it wants? On January 17, 1961, President Eisenhower, in his farewell address at the end of his eight-year presidency, made one of the most important speeches of the 20th century. Here's an excerpt:

> "A vital element in keeping the peace is our military establishment. Our arms must be mighty, ready for instant action, so that no potential aggressor may be tempted to risk his own destruction. ... This conjunction of an immense military establishment and a large arms industry is new in the American experience. ...
>
> We recognize the imperative need for this development. Yet we must not fail to comprehend its grave implications. Our toil, resources and livelihood are all involved; so is the very structure of our society. In the councils of government, we must guard against the acquisition of unwarranted influence, whether sought or unsought, by the military-industrial complex.

The potential for the disastrous rise of misplaced power exists and will persist. We must never let the weight of this combination endanger our liberties or democratic processes. We should take nothing for granted. Only an alert and knowledgeable citizenry can compel the proper meshing of the huge industrial and military machinery of defense with our peaceful methods and goals, so that security and liberty may prosper together."[58]

President Eisenhower was warning about the difficulty of calculating the cost/benefit of our military establishment, which is subject to dangerous distortions. Therefore, he suggested we proceed with great caution. And, with enormous respect for one of my favorite presidents, I think NBI makes it easier to follow President Eisenhower's advice.

Cost/benefit analyses are much easier in some areas. While there always are complicating factors, healthcare and education both need cost/benefit analysis. Those who assert that the US has the best healthcare in the world should test their statement by asking how much we spend per person per year or what percent of our total economy (gross domestic product or GDP) we spend on healthcare.

Virtually everyone agrees we spend more than any other country in the world, according to both measures. At this writing, in January 2014, the US probably just passed 18% of our GDP spent on healthcare, about 6 percentage points (one-third) higher than any other country. And, by virtually all accepted measures, we do not get adequate value for the money spent. We do not do well when cost/benefit analysis is carefully applied. According to the Organisation for Economic Co-operation and Development (OECD), an international organization known for the accuracy of its statistics:

---

58   Eisenhower, Dwight D. "Farewell Address to the Nation." Washington, DC, 17 Jan. 1961. http://mcadams.posc.mu.edu/ike.htm

"Health spending accounted for 17.6% of GDP in the United States in 2010 ... by far the highest share in the OECD, and a full eight percentage points higher than the OECD average of 9.5% ... The United States spent ... two-and-a-half times more than the OECD average ... (adjusted for purchasing power)."[59]

Education is another important example. It is fairly easy to measure how much money is spent per pupil per year. Up to a point, results also can be measured: the percentage of students who go on to college, how well they do on standardized reading and math tests, and so forth. According to the National Center for Education Statistics, in 2009-10, the United States spent $11,184 per student on elementary and secondary education, about one-third higher than the OECD average.[60] Despite higher spending on education, US students score near the OECD average in reading and science, but significantly below the average in math.[61] In 2010, approximately 68% of high school graduates went on to attend college;[62] on average, the graduation rate for US college students is 45%.[63]

We have every right to ask how much we spend per pupil and what results we get. Measuring such things is not an exact science. There are intervening factors. The point is that cost/benefit analysis should be used but its limitations acknowledged.

---

59   OECD Health Data 2012: How Does the United States Compare. OECD, 28 June 2012. Web. 31 Jan. 2013.

60   NCES. "Indicator 22: Education Expenditures by Country." *The Condition of Education* 2012.

61   Programme for International Student Assessment (PISA). What Students Know and Can Do: Student Performance in Reading, Mathematics and Science. OECD, 2010.

62   National Center for Education Statistics. Percentage of high school completers who were enrolled in two- or four-year colleges the October immediately following high school completion, by family income: 1975–2010.

63   ACT. Summary Table: National Persistence to Degree Rates by Institutional Type. 2012.

4. Peripheral Benefits Ploy (PBP)

This is a sensitive area, exemplified by Gloria-May Trapasino, whom you will meet later. Goals advocated may be unquestionably positive, but the route to reaching them can be very indirect and grossly expensive.[64] The peripheral benefits ploy is especially evident when members of the House or Senate are trying to get contracts for work performed in their districts regardless of the real need for products produced.

Keep your eye on the balls (and strikes).
Don't go to a baseball game to get a suntan.

I am old enough to remember October 1957 when the Soviet Union (Russia again today) shocked the world by launching Sputnik I, a beachball-sized satellite, into space. Along with my sister, Martha, I was riding in the back of a 1955 red-and-white Pontiac. We heard a newscast (on an AM radio) about the launch. My father—along with most Americans—could not believe it. "The damn Russian (sic) Communists might really be ahead of us," he said. Well, it was true, and the US was shaken.

Even as a little kid, I could see almost instant results, such as better science textbooks in elementary school. The government swung into action in ways not seen since the attack on Pearl Harbor on December 7, 1941. Massive new programs were formed to improve science and engineering education. A new agency—NASA—was created. On May 25, 1961, President John Kennedy, addressing Congress, showed how far we had come in four years:

First, I believe that this nation should commit itself to achieving the goal, before this decade is out, of landing a man on the moon and returning him back safely to the earth. No single space project in this

---

64 These ideas were inspired by conversations in the 1980s with my old friend and mentor, the late Professor Peter H. Rohn (1924-2011).

period will be more impressive to mankind, or more important for the long-range exploration of space; and none will be so difficult or expensive to accomplish.[65]

As everyone knows—and those of us over 50 remember firsthand—that goal was achieved on July 20, 1969, when Neil Armstrong became the first human to walk on the surface of the moon.[66]

After 1969, the space program lost much of its luster. How could you top the first moonwalk? There were other demands on the government's resources, including more robust social programs and the war in Vietnam. You guessed it—a reallocation of values occurred. It became increasingly difficult for NASA to justify its budget.

Of course, there were those who argued strongly for NASA, some who believed in space exploration as an indelible part of the American character and others who had vast NASA facilities in their states. How did NASA respond to attempts to reduce its budget? It still argued for the direct benefit of the space program but a major aspect of that, the threat from the Soviet Union, was increasingly hard to sell. So NASA and its supporters turned to what I call the:

Peripheral Benefits Ploy (PBP): justifying an action not by its primary goal but by secondary results

 They pointed to all of the secondary benefits of the space program, some of which were unexpected. Medical research was advanced. Scientific experiments impossible on earth could be carried out in the weightless environment of space. Space exploration provided the means to understand earth better, for example, more precise mapping to improve weather forecasting.

65   Kennedy, John F. "Moon Speech." Presidential Address Before a Joint Session of Congress. Washington D.C. 25 May 1961. Address.
66   See NASA website: http://history.nasa.gov/moondec.html

Another aspect of the PBP is seen in almost nonstop ads on television and the Internet. These ads push a certain industry. Pick any industry; oil and gas drilling is a good choice. The ads emphasize jobs that are related to these industries, with pictures of happy people working at these "good jobs right here in America." Sure we all want good jobs for everyone, but it is much more complicated than that: good jobs at what cost and in which areas? A nationwide prostitution business would create tens of thousands of high-paying jobs, but who advocates for that? A hundred years ago, if we had worried too much about job losses for blacksmiths, we'd still be using horses as the main mode for personal transportation. The goal of a complex, modern society should be to provide sensible rules, e.g., minimum wages, environmental standards, and fair trade, then let the marketplace decide where the jobs go.

Many of these benefits are real and should be considered, but the issue of cost must not be ignored. Each war the US has fought has improved medical care, but no one is suggesting we fight wars to improve medical care in emergency rooms! Watch carefully for the source of these PBPs. If a House of Representatives member from a district with a huge NASA facility argues especially strongly for the medical benefits of NASA programs, be extremely suspicious! I am tempted to say we should stop all discussion of peripheral benefits. That is not realistic, but we must shine a bright light on this practice.

The day before I wrote this section, CNN was interviewing a politician from Florida who was reacting to President Obama's proposed reduction of funding for the space program. What was his argument: The space program had made digital photography possible!

CHAPTER 7

THOUGHT-REVOKING WORDS

Words, words, words, I'm so sick of words.[67]

I have already confessed my love for the English language, so it might seem to you I'm getting off the point with anecdotes about my father/mother tongue. The choice of words is one of the principal weapons used to try to distract us with bull-laden information. You must be on guard for words, almost like programs on your computer that scan for viruses. There are some words that are utterly meaningless and should just be ignored, even some whose meanings have been reversed.

---

67 Song lyric from *My Fair Lady*, a musical adaptation of George Bernard Shaw's famous play, *Pygmalion*. I believe Mr. Shaw, were he alive today, would join our NBI crusade and could produce the best ARNBisms.

When I teach comparative politics, the subfield of political science concerned broadly with similarities and contrasts among the governments of the more than 190 countries in the world, I point out that you can tell almost nothing from the official name of a country. For example, Denmark, one of the most democratic countries on the planet, officially is the Kingdom of Denmark. North Korea, officially the Democratic People's Republic of Korea, has about as little democracy as one could imagine and routinely abuses its people. Your search for NBI should make you very suspicious of names and phrases.

Sometimes it seems there is an inverse relationship[68] between a name and real goal, e.g., political candidates who talk the most about reform seem to do the least to achieve it. There is a whole group of words that generally seem positive but are so broad there is no agreement on what they mean. "Reform" is one such word. People on television and the Internet seem to talk a lot about Medicare and Social Security reform. Everyone is in favor of reform, but this doesn't necessarily mean that a bill will pass Congress and be signed into law by President Obama. Why? Because the word "reform" is so broadly aspirational that there is almost no agreement on what it means.

A particularly troublesome area is advocacy groups that advertise everywhere. Some of these are above board; some have noble goals. But words are important and, more precisely in this instance, these names should be taken with a mine full of salt. There are so many of these groups, it was difficult for me to come up with a name for a hypothetical group to make my point. I think I have found one.[69]

---

68 An inverse (or negative) relationship is one where an increase in variable "A" is linked to a decrease in variable "B." On the other hand, a direct (or positive) relationship is one where an increase in variable "A" is linked to an increase in variable "B." For example, the amount of sugar consumed in a year and percentage of body fat might have a positive relationship, whereas hours spent exercising and percentage of body fat might have a negative relationship.

69 A careful Internet search found nothing in the real world that was close to this, even for the acronym CPAF.

The Center for the Preservation of American Freedoms (CPAF)

Bear in mind, CPAF (the power of acronyms!) does not really exist, but it is remarkably similar to many organizations I see on television and on the Internet every day. Often, such organizations use flashy advertisements with celebrity spokespeople soliciting money. They have every right to advocate for their cause and, within the bounds of the law, to raise money. NBI requires that the cause be made explicit. What kinds of freedoms is CPAF trying to preserve: freedom from hunger, freedom to carry guns into our churches, freedom of religion, freedom to say a Muslim prayer in public schools? You need to find out exactly what goals these organizations really have. If you look carefully and cannot understand the goals of CPAF, instead give your money to the SPoCOCP (the Society for the Preservation of Cranky Old College Professors) or if you must SMoCOCP (the Society for the Muzzling of Cranky Old College Professors).

Sometimes a word is fine in one context but total bull in another. Consider the perfectly good word "hope." Let me make it perfectly clear I am not against hope! But "hope" is a slippery little word, so much so that I call it the hedge of hope. This applies especially to politicians but also to everything from thumbtacks to senatorial campaigns.

Maybe I should not pick on the South, but shucks, somebody has to do it. Senator Pinckney Smythe (a hypothetical senator) represents the great state of South Carolina and, due to decades of seniority, he is ranking member (member from the party not holding a majority who has been there the longest) on the Senate Committee on Finance. Smythe has a lot of power for a Republican, considering the Democrats control the Senate. During a recent news conference, Senator Smythe was asked the following question by a prominent NBC reporter:

Senator, the finance committee begins hearings tomorrow and will address one of the most problematic issues of our time—reforming Medicare. As you have said, the current system is unsustainable given the increasing cost of healthcare and our aging population. Senator, let's cut to the chase. Do you think the committee will be able to agree on a set of reforms that will make Medicare solvent until the year 2040? Damn good question, if I do say so myself, to which there are three acceptable answers:

- Yes
- No
- I don't know

Senator Smythe, a wise and extremely old man (not to be confused with very wise and somewhat old), immediately sees the bind he is in. The TV cameras are rolling and 30% of voters in South Carolina are watching. If he says "yes" and the committee fails, it will look bad for him, and he will be reminded of his mistake. If he says "no," he will look ineffective and if he says he doesn't know, Smythe may look stupid. Politicians are stunningly miserly when it comes to admitting they do not know. What does Smythe say—"I hope so"? Of course he hopes so, but that completely avoids answering the question. Many reporters, even those on TV shows with take-no-prisoners sounding names, let politicians get away with this. An incredible amount of sloppy thinking sneaks through using the "hedge of hope." NBI can reduce this problem.

There is no way to anticipate all the Trojan horse words. In fact they change all the time. Permit me another medical analogy.[70] As soon as our brains develop an immune response to certain "word viruses," they mutate into other forms of word viruses. You can improve your word-alert reflexes by being on guard for certain words or phrases that often

---

70   Professor Charlotte Ku, who has been extremely helpful in reading my
      manuscripts, does not like my medical analogies. I have assured her, repeatedly,
      that she cannot contract diseases from a printed page that mentions them.

signal a flood of bull-laden information. Each of us needs a somewhat different list depending on a number of factors. I try to speak as I preach, but not always successfully, e.g., I use some of the words listed below. Here's my current but constantly expanding list.

A Few Landmine Words and Phrases

Give a 110%

All of us learned in fourth grade that the maximum value of measurable things, like grades on tests and effort in a Tiddlywinks tournament, is 100%. But many people routinely shatter the 100% ceiling of perfection. It's most blatant in sports where semi-literate $5 million a year athletes in end-of-game interviews mumble, "I came to play and gave 120% today." Why stop at 120%?

Quite frankly

Often words and phrases reverse their real meaning—up means down and down means up. Crazy, isn't it? When people are not being honest and candid with you, sometimes they will say "quite frankly." In this Alice-in-Wonderland world, "quite frankly" usually is less frank than just "frankly." Any politician who answers a question saying "somewhat frankly" automatically gets my vote.

My good friend

Obviously it is appropriate to distinguish between close and casual friends. But often politicians and salespeople use it as a way to gain your trust. It is as if they are seeking a way to accelerate the whole friendship process going from meeting to good friend in a split second. Be careful.

Lasts for 12 whole months

Advertisements, usually when talking about guarantees or rights to return a product, often modify a precise measure. Besides being stupid—is a whole 12 months longer than a year?—this kind of language often is an indication of a sleazy operation. Be careful.

Special

I'm tempted to say "special" is not special anymore. "Special" used to mean rare, important, and unusual. Now it means none of these. Some of my favorite TV series describe all of their episodes as "special." Fundraisers for charities call all potential donors "special friends." I'm declaring this book a special-free zone!

Clinical studies prove

These deceptive three words usually refer to medicines, often over-the-counter ones, that have very few restrictions on their sale. There are standards for clinical studies, but these seldom are explained or applied. Almost any claim can be made. Many recent ads brag that a medicine was "selected for a clinical trial." What did the clinical trial reveal?

Common sense

Few expressions sound better but mean less than "common sense." Recently it has been used most often by politicians who do not like the enormous changes in healthcare passed by Congress and signed into law in 2010.[71] They often say something like, "My constituents are demanding common sense solutions to healthcare." This tells you absolutely nothing; in fact, it is a cheap substitute for a thoughtful answer, like a Rolex watch case without any internal parts. Usually the

---

71 Note that I am not calling it "reform." That's a loaded word; but I do think it is an improvement.

expression is nothing more than a lazy substitute for careful consideration of a complex issue.

Encore performance

I don't remember when this started, but it has overtaken television. It makes me want to ask what damn fools do they think we are. We used to use the more accurate and clear terms "repeat" or "rerun." They hardly exist anymore. Instead we call them "encore" performances. "Encore" is the French word for "again." Do "encore" episodes of 60 Minutes stay fresh longer than reruns?

XXX dollar value

This problem is prevalent in infomercials. Often you see a product that seems to work wonderfully (pitched by someone who talks at 400 words per minute with an English accent). The person selling the product says, e.g., a $20 value, but if you order it within the next 10 minutes, you will get four of them, an incredible $80 value for only $20 plus (unspecified) shipping and handling. The idea of "value" has lost virtually all value!

Guarantee

Guarantees are supposed to protect us if a product does not perform as intended. Some are great. New car guarantees, thanks to governmental regulation and competition, have become much better. Many guarantees are utterly worthless, e.g., they have impossible conditions attached. I suspect we could find paint with a 20-year guarantee provided you scrape it off the walls and return it to the manufacturer. Many guarantees exclude "regular wear and tear," but who makes this judgment? The point is that not all guarantees are the same. Be suspicious and read the fine print to see what conditions are attached. The general rule is to buy a product that is less likely to break rather than relying on a guarantee.

Award winning

Not all awards are created equal, and many are nothing more than an advertising gimmick. Be suspicious; many "awards" mean nothing as far as the value of the product is concerned. Ask questions like: What criteria did the award committee use? Who funds the organization giving the award? How many products were considered?

As seen on television

This is so ridiculous at first I thought it was a joke. There are sections of stores, occasionally entire stores, pushing products under the proud banner "as seen on television." What does this mean? Everyone with a room temperature IQ (Fahrenheit) must agree that a vast amount of junk gets peddled on TV. How could this be a selling point? I suspect it is left over from an era when television advertising was more expensive, better regulated, and provided at least a little protection. That era is gone. God help us when your local "Super*Cheap*Mart" has a special section dedicated to products "as seen on the Internet"!

Actually

There should be a name for words whose meanings don't just shift in our vibrant English language but which now mean the opposite of the original definition. That is true for "actually." It often means people are less likely to do as they promise. When your senator says, "Actually, I fully intended to support the president on this issue," it means less, not more, chance of support. If Uncle Bud tells you, "Actually, I'm going to repay that $50 damn soon," don't count on getting the money.

Literally

"Literally" has a literal meaning. It is intended to mean something that seems unusual or even impossible really did occur. But general usage has deviated so far from the correct meaning that we'd be better off without the word. Example: "The music was awesome. It literally caused my head to explode." The point is that "literally" has become a cheap, ineffective substitute for providing a good description of what occurred.

Exponential

This word has a precise meaning in mathematics: The rate of growth (or decay) of something is proportional to its current value. It does not mean huge, which is the way it generally is used. Unfortunately it has migrated into standard English, becoming a lazy substitute for explaining the extent and nature of the change. Assume that US inflation is out of control and prices have been increasing at a 25% annual rate for 24 consecutive months with no end in sight. The TV news reader might say we have an "exponential increase" in the cost of living. That might scare people but provides little useful information. We can do much better. The 25% annual rate, if it continues, will cause prices to double in about 3½ years.

The fact of the matter is

This sneaky little phrase is used so often I am surprised we take it so seriously. The phrase is most common when someone is being challenged and has too few facts to support their opinion. Therefore, when someone says "the fact of the matter is," they are less likely to be basing their assertion on facts or are uncertain of their facts.

Sharing with you

Sharing implies that something important is being communicated between people with a personal bond between them. When my son got a post-doctoral fellowship in physics, I walked across the building and told some of my faculty colleagues. If those colleagues are people I know especially well or who know my son personally, it's fine to describe what I've done as "sharing." But increasingly sharing is used to convey any information. I've been in meetings when an academic administrator "shares" with a group of 500 that Penn State's tuition probably will increase 4% for next year. Important information? Yes. Shareworthy? Hardly. Often people "share with you" to try to get you to accept things uncritically.

With all due respect

This expression should be purged from our language. It used to mean "You are owed some respect because of your position or status." Now it really means "you've just said something idiotic, but I won't say so directly." Seldom does this signal real respect.

Exactly

This has become a filler word that has moved completely away from its real meaning. If you have an accurate watch and someone asks you for the time, it's all right to say "exactly 2:22." Today, in almost every kind of conversation, "exactly" means "I heard you," "you're a good friend," "generally I agree," or "good point." Talk shows have distorted "exactly" even further. When more than three people are talking, "exactly" often is a marker or a wedge inserted by those who are being left out of the conversation and want to re-enter it. Let's suspend the use of "exactly" for exactly a decade.

Research shows

A common ad on TV says, "Research shows cell health is important to long life." I'm glad they cleared that one up. Research also shows that falling into a whirling aircraft propeller can be hazardous to your health. The point is that the statement "research shows" seldom reflects real research, and not all research is created equal.

Playing politics

As a political scientist, I am sensitive about this expression. When have you heard one politician accuse another of "playing economics" or "playing sociology"? Politics is the art of negotiation and compromise, but the accusation "playing politics" usually means one side does not like the other and is unwilling or unable to explain why. "Playing politics" should not be a pejorative term, but it almost always is. It is supposed to imply political negotiation, but nowadays it is commonly used to accuse the opposing party of allowing partisan politics to interfere with basic principles and shared values rather than looking out for the national interest.

Rx3 # 6: Terms of Address

I tend to address people in a formal way. I believe that people should call one another by first names as an indication of friendship developed carefully and meaning something. I don't like the fact that a politician can work a crowd of 400 people, tell all of them to "call me Pinky," and many will think they've made a new friend. Salespeople can be even worse, luring you into the first-name basis trap where you get sucked into believing they are your friend and are doing you a favor by selling you that Edsel.[72] I can be fairly gutless but have always wanted to say to a pushy salesperson, "Dammit, I am not here to make you my friend. I am here only to buy this widget as quickly, painlessly, and cheaply as possible" under the protective shroud of NBI. Do yourself a favor—resist first names, and it will make it easier for you to pursue NBI. You might just improve the quality of your real friends.

---

72   Sorry, maybe this is too esoteric, but I could not resist. Edsel was a "mid-size" model introduced by Ford in 1958. It was a strange looking car that was too large for shifting American habits. It was a marketing and sales disaster lasting only three model years. The front of it looked like a fish, and the automatic transmission was shifted with buttons in the middle of the steering wheel.

CHAPTER 8

THE PITCHPERSON PROBLEM

onsider the pitchman or pitcher[73]—the person who is pitching a product or political position. This is so easy to miss. We are all human (even me), and we can get drawn in by the various techniques used by advertisers. This is the lifeblood of Madison Avenue. Let me start with a couple of general warnings and then illustrate with three distinct pitchperson problems. Congratulations—you have just witnessed the birth of an acronym: pitchperson problem (PPP). Savor the power of acronyms!

There are several huge PPPs that cut across virtually all my examples, among them sampling, compensation, and expertise, a fancy word I try not to use that means there is some reason to believe

---

73 I am not sure what the gender-neutral version of pitchman should be: pitcher or pitchperson with due apologies especially to beer-loving baseball fans.

the pitchperson knows something about the thing he/she is pitching. Think about it. In most cases, pitch people say, "I really like this deodorant" (or whatever the product is) and sometimes they also claim to use the product. What is our sample? One person, a skewed sample at that. This cannot possibly be an indication of how everyone would react to the product, service, or promise from a politician. If we kept our wits about us we'd be suspicious, but the ad agencies with their focus groups and enormous budgets try to keep one step ahead of us.

One tactic I find especially insulting is the choice of pitch people with British accents presumably because Americans, due to some remnant of insecurity dating to 1776, are impressed by this. I like Britain, teach British politics, and visit the United Kingdom often. But a British accent is no more an indication of knowledge of anything than a Southern drawl is an indication of slow thinking and lack of sophistication. Both prejudices simply are wrong.

The second broad PPP is compensation. There is an old expression— "Where you stand depends on where you sit." We might modify that to "What you're paid determines what you pitch." Was the pitchperson paid to say what S.H.It said (are you reading carefully)? Could it be that being paid an obscene amount of money to offer such high praise for the product affected the person's judgment? This is such an important issue that I am amazed how often it is overlooked.

Did the pitchperson get paid for making the pitch? It can be hard to tell. In some states and for some kinds of endorsements, the law requires that the ads disclose that this has been "a compensated endorsement," bureaucratic speak for the fact the person got paid a hell of a lot of money for making the ad. But the laws are not always obeyed and, when they are, it can be in such fine print and/or for such a brief period of time on the TV or computer screen that most people miss it.

Ask what qualifications the pitcher has to pitch.

Third, what qualifications does the pitchperson have for evaluating the product or service? We often get sucked into amazingly illogical fits between the pitchperson and the product.

Let me personalize this to make the point (stretching the bounds of good taste). I've got hammertoe, a condition where the middle joint of some of your toes sticks up too far and rubs against your shoes. It can hurt a lot. Mine is treatable with the proper shoes and orthotics (see Appendix A for medical details, test results including copies of digital high-definition foot X-rays, and a photo of me ballet dancing [just kidding]). Seven years ago, when my hammertoe got worse, whom did I go to for advice? Thunk, thunk, thunk as Winnie the Pooh, my favorite philosopher, might say. Why not keep an eye out for an infomercial in which a former poet laureate of the US enthusiastically endorses her line of foot care products that promises to cure not only hammertoe but also bunions, warts, flat feet, and sciatica? I like poetry (I even use some in my final chapter) but shouldn't I treat my hammertoe first by asking my primary care physician and then perhaps by seeing a podiatrist? This example is not farfetched; the crap to which we are subjected suggests that many advertisers think we are pea-brained idiots.

Below I describe three hypothetical examples that are frighteningly similar to PPPs that appear on TV and the Internet all the time.

Hypothetical PPP # 1–
a world famous, retired, professional athlete
Name of Pitchperson: Willi Strong

Mr. Strong played 12 years as a running back in the National Football League and still holds records for the most yards gained in one season and second for career yardage. Strong led his team, the Meadville Rabid Dogs, to three Super Bowl championships. The team colors of the Rabid Dogs are dark brown and bright red. Huge numbers of football fans recognize Strong and remember him in his brown-and-red uniform wearing number 50, a number since retired. Mr. Strong's average salary was more than $8 million per year. He invested his money wisely and, five years after his retirement, still receives large sums from endorsements. His stable of nine cars includes a 2010 Maybach (sort of a super Mercedes-Benz) 62S that is more than 20 feet long and cost almost half a million dollars! You get the picture.

The Pitch:

Mr. Strong is standing in front of a pretty summer country scene with trees and a stream in the background. He is wearing his Rabid Dogs jersey (who can forget those shades of red and brown?), still showing the legendary number 50. Strong says the following during a 40-second commercial:

"This is your friend Willi Strong. I'll never forget the support of millions of you fans even before the Rabid Dogs rose to the top of the NFL. I know something about strong and even more about the number 50. (pauses and smiles knowingly) That's why I want to recommend Strong Trash Bags. They hold 50 gallons and are 50% stronger than the leading brand. How about those numbers! (Points a bit sheepishly to the #50 on his shirt) Come to think of it, I love the color of these Strong bags. (points to the bag that is the same color as the brown of his jersey) I recommend Strong Trash Bags. And remember, when the trash has to go, be Strong."

Hypothetical PPP # 2–a Harvard Ph.D. in organic chemistry
Name of Pitchperson: Templeton Fettenseigger

Dr. Fettenseigger is perhaps the most widely known organic chemist in the world. After getting his Ph.D. from Harvard, he did post-doctoral work at the University of Chicago. He began his teaching and research career at Princeton University, where he rose quickly through the ranks, and by age 36 was a full professor. At age 40 he was awarded a prestigious endowed professorship. In 2005 he received the Nobel Prize in chemistry for his work on chiral synthesis of complex molecules. Unlike many famous scientists, Dr. Fettenseigger has been willing and effective at explaining science to a lay audience. He has appeared on many television shows including *Jimmy Kimmel Live*, *The Daily Show with Jon Stewart*, and *60 Minutes*.

The Pitch:

It begins with a solemn male voice with an upper-class English accent saying, "Dr. Templeton Fettenseigger is one of the leading scientists of our time. His scientific research accomplishments have been acclaimed the world over culminating in 2005 when Dr. Fettenseigger received the Nobel Prize." (video of Fettenseigger in white tie and tails receiving the prize from the king of Sweden in one of the most formal ceremonies existing in the modern world). The video switches to Fettenseigger in tennis attire, racket in hand next to a tennis court. He says:

"This is Templeton Fettenseigger. I am sure some of you don't recognize me dressed for my favorite sport, tennis. I've spent my life deciphering the wonders of science. I hope my television specials and books have helped you and your children to develop a love of science. Tennis is the kind of exercise I use to keep my mind and body healthy—it makes me a better scientist. Recently arthritis in my knees and shoulder made tennis almost impossible. I wanted to avoid taking medications because of possible severe side effects and, for me, surgery is the last resort. Then a friend in my lab told me she had superb results with Arthrit-Be-Gone a cream you apply directly to painful joints. I was skeptical, but tried it and the results 'play for themselves.' "

Video switches to Fettenseigger beginning a vigorous game of tennis with a woman. The solemn British accent tells you how to order Arthrit-Be-Gone online.

Hypothetical PPP # 3—world-famous singer, TV, and movie star with a personal link to a disease

Name of Pitchperson: Gloria-May Trapasino

Ms. Trapasino is one of the most famous actresses in the world and still going strong at age 54. She is from Ohio and attended the prestigious Oberlin College, majoring in music. Unlike many in the entertainment world, she has led a squeaky-clean personal life, has been married to the same man for 30 years, not a single scandal, hardly even any negative media coverage. Everyone seems to love and respect Ms. Trapasino. She has won two Oscars for movie musicals and prestigious awards for her work on Broadway and the West End in London. Ms. Trapasino and her husband, Elihu McElroy, have two children, a son, age 28, and a daughter, who died a year ago from the rare disease $\Lambda\Xi\Omega$. Ms. Trapasino has set up a foundation to support research in $\Lambda\Xi\Omega$.

The Pitch:

Ms. Trapasino, dressed formally, beautifully, and conservatively, is standing in the study of her Beverly Hills home. Her husband is sitting next to her in a dark-red leather armchair. She says:

"Ladies and gentlemen, this is Gloria-May Trapasino. I am here in my Los Angeles home with the love of my life, my husband of 30 years, Elihu. (The two look lovingly at each other.) I should like to tell you about the most important role of my long career. Our beloved daughter, Beverly, died a year ago of $\Lambda\Xi\Omega$; she was only 25 years old, just beginning her journey as an adult. Like most people who contract this dreadful disease, Beverly was struck young, at age 5. We could afford the best medical care in the world, including treatment at a world famous clinic in Vienna, Austria. But $\Lambda\Xi\Omega$ is relentless. Beverly's body and mind—but not her soul—began to slip away by the time she was 12. Today my husband and I are announcing that we are contributing $50 million to create the Trapasino Foundation for the Treatment and Cure of $\Lambda\Xi\Omega$. I hope you will join us in this fight."

Next the video switches to a famous medical researcher who works for the Trapasino Foundation. He confirms how devastating this disease is and how, for the first time, "a cure seems possible." Next complete details about your tax-deductible contribution are provided along with videos of researchers and physicians, in white coats, treating ΛΞΩ patients.

This Pitchperson Problem—PPP—cannot be cured. But an effective NBI program can do a much better job of controlling it. And pitch people cannot be outlawed; in a free society, that cure would be worse than the disease. Sure, there should be meaningful regulations, but these are hard to draft and even harder to enforce. The best defense is an informed public applying the principles outlined here. This is a major reason I wrote this book.

All pitches are not created equal. Some are just silly and can be dismissed out of hand. If a PP says you can safely lose 15 pounds in five days following the miracle Styrofoam pellet diet, the numbers simply do not add up. Losing one pound means you have to burn 3,500 calories. How do you do that? It's so simple to state but so hard to do. Eat less and exercise (move) more. You cannot safely burn 10,000 calories a day unless you run a marathon.

Cases like my hypothetical Gloria-May Trapasino are so sensitive and complex, I was hesitant to include it, but they are a reality that should be understood. In most cases, they mean well and many do wonderful work. If I were in that tragic situation, I might do exactly the same thing. It sounds cold and unfeeling, but is this the most intelligent way to allocate our money for medical research? Does anyone have the right to intervene and limit how Ms. Trapasino spends her money so long as she earned it and spends it legally?

This is heavy-duty authoritative allocation of values. What values should the US government allocate when it comes to situations like these three hypothetical PPPs? I suspect most Americans would say we have freedom to spend money however we wish, and government should stay out of those decisions. Others would say it's not that simple. Do potential buyers of Strong Trash Bags have a right to know if Mr. Strong has been paid for his enthusiastic endorsement?

CHAPTER 9

Tactics: Putting NBI into Practice

Explaining the Approach

One of the greatest strengths of NBI and why I am so optimistic about making a difference is the ease with which you can give voice and action to our frustrations in the face of the ridiculous information bombarding us from all directions and on myriad kinds of devices. I am not saying that NBI will quickly cure all of the problems the US faces in the second decade of the 21st century. We can't force all the fast-talking car salesmen into the priesthood.[74] But there is

---

74 Sorry, maybe this is a bad example in this modern era. Yes, I believe the priesthood should be open to women.

plenty we can do, many strategies and room for millions of Americans to participate even though they have very different interests, beliefs, and comfort zones. These strategies are not abstractions; they are concrete things you can do immediately. Perhaps most important, these strategies can be adapted to your individual situation and lifestyle. One size does not have to fit all. Some of you will be uncomfortable wearing an Arnbi T-shirt as you shop at a mall; others might want to dress the whole family in Arnbi clothes.

 Grassroots NBI movement:
Different shovels for different folks

In the pages that follow, I've provided specific tools to use against some of the most extreme examples of NBI deficiency: 18 NBI Guidance Cards to help you to deal more effectively with everything from politicians to supermarkets. I've developed two kinds of Guidance Cards.[75]

The NBI Guidance Survey CARD describes the lay of the land and provides advice in these nine broad areas:

- Reducing noise and clutter
- Sampling
- Word warnings
- Vested interests
- Labels
- Money and credit
- Politicians and politics
- Healthcare
- Television

---

75 NBI Guidance Cards help you to assess (judge) and access (get to the meaning of) politicians' speeches.

The NBI Guidance Focus CARD hones in on these nine specific NBI trouble spots:

- Infomercials
- Supermarket
- Credit
- Car
- Cell
- Airline
- Magazine
- Voting
- College

You may have noticed I write the name of a guidance card somewhat differently because I have found it helpful to distinguish between the versions.

- For the Survey Card, the word "card" zooms out like this— CARD—indicating a broader focus.
- For the Focus Card, the word "card" zooms in like this—**CARD** —showing the narrower focus.

I must give proper credit; this stunningly creative idea came to me in a dream in which Arnbi spoke to me. His wisdom remains fresh after 2,500 years!

I can't provide guidance cards for everything you might encounter, but this two-level approach can be adapted to a wide range of activities. Remember, NBI is a new way of thinking about many aspects of your life. Once you get the hang of it, the approach can become second nature; you will be able to apply it automatically in many situations.

I suspect some of you may be thinking, "OK, Dr. Gamble has identified a real problem, but it is too big to tackle. Powerful business interests and entrenched politicians will squelch any effort to change the *status quo*."[76] That is a good point but one that can be overcome. If enough people get involved, we can use the marketplace openly and honestly.

Let me use the concrete example I know best—myself. It's 3 p.m. on a weekday, and I'm at home writing this chapter. As I write, I glance across the room to the stack of today's mail. There is an "extremely urgent" letter from *Time* magazine. As I mentioned earlier, I enjoy *Time* and have been "reading" it before I could read. But the letter is disguised to look like an urgent warning. It makes it seem as if my *Time* subscription will expire by sundown. I must immediately renew for five years or I will be permanently banned, not only from subscribing to *Time* but also from reading it. Time Warner has its ways to check on such things! Their subscription police will follow me even to my dentist's office. What can I do? There is a focus NBI Guidance Card for magazine subscriptions to help you efficiently evaluate and communicate our displeasure. If enough people tell *Time* they are not renewing and will switch to *The Economist* unless all renewal notices tell them in big, bold print exactly when their current subscription expires, things will change.

Here's another example. I need to run to Walmart to pick up some Omega-3 fish oil. To be more efficient, I take my focus NBI Guidance Card for supermarkets to make notes on how Walmart is doing in a number of areas, such as clear unit pricing, shelf labels that are legible even to less-than-young eyes, and defining precisely what a serving size is.

The point is that tens of millions of individual actions taken by millions of Americans can make a difference. Perhaps a single complaint will not make any difference. I think I am pretty clever and

---

76 "Status quo" is a very useful Latin expression meaning "present or current situation.

can talk a convincing game, but it can be hard to get through to a real person, let alone someone who has authority. But if enough people act—and NBI Guidance Cards show you how—things have a better chance of changing

The cynics among you may be thinking any improvement will not last—the unscrupulous side of business soon will rear its ugly head, and we will return to teaser mortgage rates, billion-dollar bailouts, and advertised airline fares that hide half of the real cost. I am more optimistic. I think we can turn the tide so that more businesses will concentrate on making and selling products of the highest quality rather than using trickery to get us to waste our money on worthless, misrepresented, and grossly overpriced products. Of course, there always will be snake-oil salespeople, but we can reduce their influence. Arnbi versus a snake-oil salesperson is no contest!

 **Cramming a 168-page book into 380 pages is easy to do but it wastes time, trees, and diminishes understanding.**

Some cards may be of little value to you. If you always pay cash for a car, you don't need a focus card on automobile financing. The cards can't cover every possible contingency, but many of the concepts explained earlier will help you to deal with many different situations. For example, the list of word viruses can be like a Geiger counter providing advanced warning of impending bull-laden information. The guidance cards work like training wheels on a bicycle; once you get the hang of them, they will transport you to better information and eventually you can discard those training wheels.

There is another dimension to guidance cards that goes to the heart of NBI. NBI seeks to change the contours of American political and economic life by gradually, but significantly, raising the standards of information provided. Remember, this is a grassroots effort in which everyone can participate according to individual needs, interests, and available time. I'm relying on an army of retired or semi-retired, senior or semi-senior citizens who have the time and interest to get involved. And their interest can be aimed at a broad range of NBI issues from (1) getting rid of prices like $9.99 to (2) requiring the disclosure of the real terms of a mortgage.

Don't feel bad if you don't have time to use all the guidance cards. If you are a twenty-something single parent struggling to make ends meet, relax, understand, and use the principles explained here and let the older generation take care of the foot soldier work. Once they succeed, the new, better information environment will benefit all of us, a rising tide of NBI with Arnbi as captain of the ship.

I am going to begin with survey cards because it seems logical to start with more general situations to set the stage for the more concrete focused cards. However, these may have less bearing on your day-to-day life, so skip ahead as needed.

Survey CARDs

The scope of the survey cards that follow is broad. You should already be prepared to use them. For most people, the survey cards are best used in the comfort of your home (as the expression goes). Take them to bed with you. Keep them in your lap as you watch TV and don't be surprised if they are used almost as much as the remote control. They help you to hone general skills to cope with our cluttered, deceptive, oversimplified information environment. They can become second nature as you confront information.

The two kinds of cards complement each other. For example, there is a focus card on buying cell phones, everyone's favorite experience just behind going to the dentist. There are dozens of "hints" from the nine survey cards that can help you deal with cell phone shopping, but these don't replace the more detailed information on the cell phone focus card. Just a few examples:

- focus on the main goal (noise and clutter card)
- "give 110%", "$ value," "actually" (word warnings card)
- "out-the-door price" (labels card)

I can't stress too strongly that each of us has different information needs (and ways you can contribute to the mass NBI effort). The nine survey cards help to put you in the proper frame of mind to deal with the nine focus cards that follow after the survey cards.

NBI Guidance Survey CARD
REDUCING NOISE AND CLUTTER

ARNBism: Reduce the noise and you can hear Adam Smith sing.

The Point: This is perhaps the broadest guidance card. American life has become so noisy, so cluttered with confusing, deceptive "information" that it can be difficult or impossible to see the core, the really important elements. You cannot stop all the noise, but below are some ways to reduce the distracting noise and clutter to improve your chances of getting information that enables you to make wiser decisions.

Keep your eye on the goal—examples: buying a good car, selecting the right senator, shopping, and so forth.

What is your main goal? _____

Essential to achieving the main goal: _____

Helpful in achieving the main goal:_____

Peripheral to achieving the main goal: _____

Danger signs for excess noise and clutter; check all that apply and watch for them.

_____ uses of the "nines" such as $9.99

_____ small print in papers or on the screen

_____ total price not given

_____ no option to buy just one item

_____ loud, repetitious pitchperson

_____ irrelevant famous person (remember Willi Strong)

_____ British accent and/or fast talking

_____ fake patriotic company/organization names, such as Liberty, Freedom & God Insurance Co.

_____ phony rewards ("units" or "points," the value of which is deceptive)

_____ testimonials (from someone like "Carol C. from California, who lost 25 pounds on the miracle Styrofoam pellet diet")

NBI Guidance Survey CARD
SAMPLING

ARNBism: Sampling problems are everywhere—find and expose them.

The Point: This is vital to NBI; it's so basic yet so often overlooked. We tend to concentrate on blatantly false information, ignoring information that may be true in a narrow sense but ignores sampling. Put simply, this means asking how typical and how representative a piece of information is. Two examples among millions:

1. the woman who wins $10 million in a state lottery
2. the businessman who states, "I started dirt poor and built a fortune worth $5 billion"

Write down the situation you suspect has a sampling problem:

_____

_____

Example: Dr. Fettenseigger endorsing Arthrit-Be-Gone for arthritis pain (see pitcher problems, Chapter 8.)
Write down exactly what claim is made:

_____

_____

Evaluation questions:
Is the sample size made explicit? Yes___ How large? _____ No _____
Is information provided about a random sample? _____
Nature of endorser (pitchperson):
Expert _____ Celebrity _____ Unclear _____ Silly____

After completing the above, put the "fact" into context. Write a brief assessment of the sample issue, forcing yourself to think about it. For example, odds of winning the lottery versus money the average person spends on tickets.

_____

_____

NBI Guidance Survey CARD
WORD WARNINGS

ARNBism: It's not quite like Pinocchio's nose, but there are clear signals.

The Point: There are many words and phrases that can serve as red flags, warning you of bull-laden information. Being on the alert will improve your odds. These can steer you in the right direction.

Hedge of hope: The word "hope" blocks vast amounts of accurate information. I hope for immortality, happiness for everyone, and world peace.

Acronym creep: SOS. Acronyms can lure you into accepting bad information. If you do not know what an acronym means, ask. And don't assume the acronym user knows anything.

Give a 110%: 100% is the maximum even for professional athletes who suffered multiple blows to the head.

Quite frankly: Sometimes words and phrases reverse their actual meaning. "Quite frankly" is less "frank" than "frankly."

12 whole months: Another kind of clutter, as distinct from 12 half-months or partial months!

Common sense: Really important but widely abused. Politicians calling for "common sense" seldom have a clue what should be done. Real common sense is uncommon.

XXX $ value: Stores can set their price, but we get to decide the value. A "$100 value for $20" plus double shipping and handling makes Arnbi cry.

Guarantee: Guarantees are supposed to protect us from products that do not perform as they are supposed to. Many are just advertising gimmicks. Read the fine print.

Actually: Another meaning reversal. "Actually, Scarlet, I love you" means Scarlet should question the love. Actually, I have trouble with "actually." "Actually" often is used when people have too much time to talk and too little to say.

Literally: "Literally" means something really did occur. No, the news did not literally blow my mind!

Exponential: Has a precise meaning in mathematics, but usually it is used to mean "very large" by someone who is too lazy or ignorant to explain "really big."

The fact of the matter is: A sneaky little phrase. Be suspicious of "facts" delivered this way.

Sharing with you: Careful—this often means someone is trying to make you accept things uncritically by treating you like an old friend.

My good friend: Friendship is precious. Often it is forced or faked to sell you a car or a juicer, or to get your vote.

Centrism creep: This always has been a problem, but it's getting much worse. Instead of understanding how to do something, skip to the desired result. Examples: student-centered colleges, patient-centered healthcare. Both are important goals but are difficult to achieve.

NBI Guidance Survey CARD
VESTED INTERESTS

ARNBism: So common, so important, yet so often ignored.

The Point: This is so important, I wish we had NBI eyeglasses that would automatically alert us to the vested interest of most information providers. Some are obvious—Straight-Shootin' Sam's Used Car Emporium exists to sell you a used car. Other examples of vested interest are far subtler, often deceptive. I'm a college professor. As such, I have a vested interest in higher education, good pay for professors, more government money, and so forth. But don't go too far. I am not suggesting you ask what vested interest your favorite grandmother has. Grandmotherly love gets a pass from me. Here is a framework for handling vested interests.

Cut to the chase. What is the vested interest? Watch the peripheral benefits ploy. Example: selling you a reverse mortgage from XYZ Finance, etc.

_____

Is the vested interest openly acknowledged: Yes___ No___

How might the vested interest conflict with your getting accurate, complete information (NBI):

_____

_____

The above should help you to assess any vested interest issue. Perhaps only a minor adjustment will be required. The following tests will help alert you to major vested interest problems.

_____ Is compensation based on your buying or doing something?

_____ Is friendship intermingled with the business or professional goal?

_____ Will the service offered improve any aspects of your life?

_____ Blurred roles—too broad, what service is provided: lawyer? medical adviser? cook?

_____ Are costs explicitly acknowledged? "Free" usually isn't!

NBI Guidance Survey CARD
LABELS

ARNBism: Buy any crap you want, but demand to know what crap you're buying.

The Point: This should be easy but often is neglected. Demand clear labels (full disclosure) for everything you buy or decisions you make. If they are not provided, avoid the product, service, candidate, or college education. The label on mayoral candidate Wellington Forsythe is harder to assess than the label on a can of Campbell's Soup. However, the "rules" shown below apply in many areas.

- If you can't see or hear it, nothing else matters. You should not have to strain your eyes to read a label or ask to see a list of donors for a political candidate.
  Visible/audible?_____
- Where it is made? I'm in favor of buying American, but in the global economy, not everything can be made in the US, especially if we want other countries to buy our stuff.
  Clearly specified? _____
- What does it contain? There should be no fine print. All the basic information must be presented (on the front of the can, TV screen, etc.
  Contents clearly specified?_____
- What is the total cost to get the good or service? We need a much higher standard. What is the out-the-door (O-t-d) cost per unit? If the airline quotes a price for one way that requires a round-trip purchase, switch to an airline that does not.
  O-t-d and unit price specified? _____

- We must not only have clear, complete labels but also demand their use in many more situations. Examples: restaurant menus, individual packaged food items.

  Is the label clear? Complete? _____

"Vote" with your actions! Don't buy the item, support the candidate, etc.

NBI Guidance Survey CARD
MONEY AND CREDIT

ARNBism: Everybody knows there are no free lunches. There also is no free money.

The Point: There are countless schemes that make it seem as if you can get money for free. Sorry—you can't. We have to pay to use someone else's money, just as we have to pay to live in someone else's apartment—it's called rent. These are some of the most flagrant ways the real cost of money is hidden.

Make no payment for three years. This kind of come-on is common for things such as furniture and home improvements, and it can be a minefield. The first problem is that it encourages buying something on credit over an extended period of time, even if you do not need to do so. The second is that they don't tell you how much the payments are after the three years; you must ask. The third is that interest may accumulate interest during those three years, and that's also something you need to ask about. Often it is a terrible deal.

Buy this car at 0% interest for six years. Occasionally this can be a good deal, particularly when auto manufacturers provide financial incentives to the dealers. Usually you can buy that dream car for much less money if you paid cash. A car that can be bought for $23,500 might cost $27,000 if you take that 0% APR loan. If you must finance your car—and try not to—don't assume the dealer's rate is the best.

Sign up for our new credit card with an introductory interest rate of 0% on all balances transferred, plus no annual fee for the card. American households with credit card debt average about $15,500 spread among several cards. The interest alone on this is probably more than $225 a month. You must consider how much the card costs per year, what the interest rate is, and when it starts. That 0% rate may go to 20% quickly and at the bank's whim. Even given the better protection provided in recent laws, it is far too easy to get trapped.

You've won the lottery (or have an annuity) that pays you $1,000 a month for 10 years. Why should you wait for your money? This example would pay you $120,000 (before taxes) over 10 years. If you want all your money now, you'll get much less, probably not even half. State lotteries contribute to the confusion by advertising "million-dollar" winners—the million dollars is probably $4,000 a month for 20 years but much less if you want a lump sum now. Some advertisers offer to help you to get your money now; demand to know exactly what percent of that million you'd get.

Even though you are 82 years old, you still can get life insurance without a physical exam. There is no medical exam required, you cannot be turned down, and it costs only $3.22 per unit per month. And your favorite TV star endorses it! There are good insurance companies offering decent programs. There also are plenty of places offering crap. If you are 82, you are a poor risk, especially if the company can't assess your health. Also, what the hell is a unit? Read the fine print and remember these companies sell insurance—they do not serve free lunches! Often they are poorly regulated.

Income tax credit for installing solar panels on your house. There are thousands of tax breaks in the US tax code for individuals and corporations. I'd get rid of all of them, but at the very least, we must realize that a tax credit is not free and that politicians must tell us how much it costs government in lost revenues. Also, ask yourself why people should need a tax credit to do the right thing. Many tax breaks do not cover the entire cost. It's like buying an expensive gadget you do not need just because it is 50% off.

NBI Guidance Survey CARD
POLITICIANS AND POLITICS

ARNBism: Plato's philosopher-king idea did not work out so well. However, you can send "Write it up, Roy" back to his used car lot in Peoria.

The Point: A little truth in advertising—as a political science professor, I'm hardly an objective observer in this area. Politics in democracies is about compromise. The process can be lengthy and inefficient. But this does not mean all politicians are corrupt and selfish. There are bad politicians, even a small percentage who should be in jail. Politicians do not have to sell their souls, but most need to accept the "beauty of gray." The following NBI-related principles will help you to deal with the complex and frustrating realm of politics. Check each item below to indicate you've considered it carefully.

____ Be adequately informed: Citizens have to be willing to spend some time to become familiar with major political issues. You should not ignore the political world just because it seems unsavory.

____ Watch your political party legacy: Chances are you adopted the political party of your parents. Take a hard look at whether this fits you at the present time.

____ Value political experience: Politics is different. Success in business or the military does not necessarily make an effective political leader.

____ Watch for vague statements: Politicians who attempt to simplify complex issues with sweeping statements seldom understand the issues well enough to explain them.

____ Watch the rhetoric: Leaders often must inspire, as when FDR said, "The only thing we have to fear is fear itself." But inspiration is not enough. President Reagan's "shining city on a hill" was vulnerable to landslides.

___ Balance local and national interests: Elected officials do serve the folks back home, but they also must consider broader national interests, especially in a globalizing world.

___ Admit they do not know: Politics is complicated, and no one can know it all. Prudent "I don't know" responses are a good sign.

___ Deplore the cost of running for office: Elective politics in the US costs far too much money. Candidates should acknowledge this fact and publish the source of all their contributions.

___ Be on the lookout for simple, quick solutions: Democracies usually act slowly and require approval at multiple levels, whereas Mussolini made the trains run on time and Hitler cured the economic depression in Germany. How did that work out for the world?

NBI Guidance Survey CARD
HEALTHCARE

ARNBism: Any medical system in which pharmacies give away prescription antibiotics and hospitals charge $5 for one aspirin must be placed under the NBI microscope.

The Point: This is the biggest economic, moral, and social issue facing the US today. The issue is too big to address in this book yet too important to ignore. By any valid measures, our system is the most expensive in the world. At least 20 countries spend less and get better results! All I can do here is offer some advice on how to drive along the pothole-ridden road that is the current system. It takes a two-page guidance card! This is not easy, and it can kill you. The Affordable Care Act, also known as Obamacare, is making the situation somewhat better.

The Basic Rule: Do you have (or are you eligible for) reasonably priced good-coverage health insurance? Usually this means a large, progressive employer, working for government at some level, or qualifying for a government-run program such as Medicare or the Veterans Health Administration.

If your answer is "no" you are in a very tough position, but you still can improve your odds by following some of the suggestions below.

A few suggestions for navigating the riptide and potholes of US healthcare.
- beware of private companies offering "quality coverage" for about $2 per day
- demand explanation of jargon: co-pay, co-insurance, pre-existing condition
- be sure your physician understands your "insurance condition"

- there is good information: Consumer Reports, most government agencies
- ask for help/explanations from your employer, insurance co., etc.
- if you do not get a clear answer, keep asking and take notes
- find a knowledgeable person and use her/him
- complain, loudly but politely, to TV, newspapers, blogs, etc.
- compare and question the prices you are charged—there are vast differences
- write to your legislator, (state and federal)—they can help

A few rules for finding a good physician. Check when you've completed each.

- ask your friends' advice and ask many different people—sample size!!
- get to know the staff in the office, remember them, call them by name
- be polite to the physician; have a list of questions ready to ask
- rating websites can be useful, but look for vested interests and sample size, and read carefully
- try to figure out who really runs the office, and use this information to your advantage
- let them see you are taking notes, but also acknowledge how challenging their job is
- don't expect your physician to be God; they are not!
- note the sequence of people you see; often it's the nurse and physician's assistant first
- bring a list of all medications and a summary of your last couple of appointments
- don't expect the physician to have perfect memory of previous visits
- don't confuse bedside manner with medical competence

NBI Guidance Survey CARD
TELEVISION

ARNBism: We need a new kind of interactive television that empowers the viewer.

The Point: Television has been in most American homes since the 1950s. I remember it well. My father—who loved new technology—bought the first set in our neighborhood in Meadville, Pennsylvania. The set cost $595 ($3,000 in today's dollars, a huge "investment" for us!), required a 60-foot high antenna, and got one snowy channel. Except for the cost of the TV set itself, in most ways, we pay drastically more today and get less. Ask yourself how many useful stations you receive. I receive about 250 stations. Recently I counted and 100 (40%) are constant advertisements. Think about it: You are paying for ads for products, and the merchants also are paying the TV provider. Talk about a sweet deal.

Assess your situation. Are you reasonably pleased with your current TV setup, both what you get and how much it costs? Be sure you remember how much it costs—automatic billing obscures this. If your answer is yes, skip to the last section.

Those who are really ticked off: The chances are very great you can get your TV either via cable or satellite. You've got to decide whether to try to improve upon or abandon cable/satellite. If you're reasonably good with computers—or know a teenager who is—and have good high-speed Internet, you probably can ditch your cable/satellite in favor of digital local channels coupled with programs streamed over the Internet. There is a lot available fairly cheaply, but it will take some hassle and might not have everything you are accustomed to.

Welcome to the crusaders' club! You have elected to try to improve your television delivery service. Here are things you can do that probably will get you more for less:

- Call your company and talk to a sales agent. Tell them you are dissatisfied and thinking about switching. They really will want to keep you. Try to get more channels at a guaranteed rate for a longer time along with other features like high definition, more sets, and DVR memory space.
- After you get a new, better deal, it's time to broaden your efforts for the greater good. Note: Even if you have not switched to a different provider, you can participate here. Bombard your provider telling them you need these changes. We won't get all of them but can shake things up by requesting the following:
  - a list of all channels you get with information about type including 24/7 ad channels
  - a bill that shows the actual, total cost per month, no "9s" and no hidden or obscure charges, e.g., taxes and extra profit fees must not be obscured by words like "provider imposed fees!"
  - on-screen information about repeats (encores!), paid programming, and compensation for endorsers
  - that the old-time networks (ABC, CBS, NBC) stop coordinating their commercial breaks; that is a restraint of trade and illegal under US antitrust law
  - a reduction in your bill based on the percent of time you did not get good quality pictures due to glitches

NBI Guidance Focus CARD
INFOMERCIALS

ARNBism: If it's that good, they'll tell you exactly how much S/H costs.

The Point: These are thin-ice ventures, so be careful! Ask yourself if you really need the product. Alternatively, you always can view them as humorous fairytales.

If you decide to go ahead, apply these tests to score. "X" all that apply and count the "X's."

1. Does the pitch person have a British accent?   _____
2. How fast does the pitchperson talk? fast: X; very fast: XX   _____
3. Are you urged to buy immediately?   _____
4. Is there a celebrity with no credentials?   _____
5. Cost of S/H not specified? Add XX   _____
6. Guarantee not mentioned or less than 30 days?   _____
7. Is the disclaimer message too small, too low volume,   _____
   too brief, or too fast to be understood? max: three X's
8. How often is "value" mentioned? one X each time   _____
9. Do the prices end in nines, e.g., $9.99?   _____
10. Is there a "full refund" with S/H deducted?   _____
    X if there is one S/H, XX if there are two
11. Delivery time not specified, add XX,   _____
    more than four weeks, add X

Total number of X's: _____

Interpretation:
- more than 13: no way—Arnbi would cry!
- 7-13: risky—consider cost carefully
- 0-6: might be OK, but this remains dangerous territory!

NBI Guidance Focus CARD
SUPERMARKET SHOPPING

ARNBism: Put your store on the miracle NBI diet.

The Point: Everyone's favorite pastime is food shopping, right? Maybe not. It's hardly surprising you'd have a guidance card. There is a lot of competition among stores, so you should be able to leverage your NBI power. I concentrate on suggestions for getting better value and clearer labels rather that telling you what to buy. Some people are on an especially tight budget, and all of us occasionally will have to stop at the local "Gas and Gulp" where we pay far too much for a gallon of milk.

Peripheral benefits ploy: Stores including Giant Eagle, where I do most of my shopping, have many inducements that have little direct relationship to getting what you want at good prices. In Giant Eagle's case, buying groceries can save you money on gasoline, and buying gas can save you money on groceries. That's fine, but it's peripheral to buying your groceries at the lowest price. Keep your eye on the avocados and the tomatoes.

How much does it really cost? Stores are drastically different than when I first entered a grocery store holding my mother's hand and saw a loaf of Wonder Bread for 19¢. There are some regulations about posting prices, but these can be confusing. Be on the lookout for the following and complain or find a new store if the practice does not change:

- Tiny confusing numbers—not clear which product price they are.
- Unclear unit and total prices: it should be obvious what a unit is and how many are in the bag. One of my pet peeves is in the

continued on next two pages...

sale of K-Cups, individual coffee pods. It's good coffee, but my Walmart provides only the price per ounce, not per K-Cup.

- Is an item priced something like four for $7? If so, the sign must tell you how much each item costs ($1.75 in this case) and if you must buy four to get this price. This strategy is often used to trick the consumer into buying more of a product, even though they would get the same price if they bought fewer. Paying attention to unit prices when grocery shopping may save you a lot of money. By comparing the unit prices of different-sized packages or brands of the same product, you will know which will give you a bigger bang for your buck.

What's in it and where does it come from?

Clear, legible labels, and signs showing you:
- country of origin
- if the product is FDA-certified organic
- if the product has been genetically modified

Federal rules provide a good start on food/nutritional information, including calories, total fat, sodium, total carbohydrates, protein, and sugar. But NBI wants to improve on these in several ways:
- insist that information on the back of food packages is clear and easily readable, including serving size
- demand labels on small packages sold as a group—the is no room on a single M&M, but there is on a 4" x 6" bag of cookies!

Create a new NBI standard for food labels that appear on the front of the package and say, "See reverse side for complete information." Offer nutritional information for both the serving size and the whole container.

Here is a proposed example for the front of a box of cookies:

	Serving (2 cookies)	Container (12 cookies)
Calories	140	840
Total fat	7g (11%)*	42g (66%)
Sodium	60mg (3%)	360mg (18%)
Carbohydrates	18g (6%)	108g (36%)
Sugars	9g	54g

* Percent Daily Values are based on a 2,000 calorie diet. See reverse of package for full nutritional information.

NBI Guidance Focus CARD
CREDIT CARDS

ARNBism: Credit cards often are a financial trap likely to catch the most vulnerable.

The Point: This is part of "money" but deserves its own card. People get sucked into using credit cards without considering the implications. As mentioned earlier, the average American household with credit card debt has about $15,500 spread among several cards. This would cost you well over $200 a month just in interest—scary!

Broad Goals:
- minimize number of cards
- zero balance on all of them—this may seem too ambitious, but Americans should see how much of their balance they can pay off, not what the maximum amount credit card companies will allow

Your situation—which best describes you?
- You can afford to pay your entire balance each month.
- You often need credit cards to make it to your next paycheck.

If you're in the "next paycheck" category, don't select credit cards because of things like airline miles, cash back, etc., because the odds are you'll lose far more in interest charges and other fees than you gain in cash back, bonus "points," and frequent traveler miles.

Specific rules to be followed to control the cards—check when completed.

___ List all your credit cards with current balances, annual interest rate, and annual cost.

___ Evaluate how clear/complete information is for each credit card bill. It should show (in big letters) new balance, minimum payment, due date, payoff time if you make only the minimum payment.

___ What "perks" does each card offer? Read carefully—"points" and "miles" depend completely on what you get and how it can be used.

___ Be careful of balance transfer offers. Often these provide no interest for a certain period of time, but you get hit with a very high rate later on.

___ Be very careful of department store and other specialty cards. Often these lure you in with a big discount on an initial purchase in the hope that later you'll carry large balances at high interest rates.

NBI Guidance Focus CARD
CAR BUYING

ARNBism: The American love affair with the automobile can be controlled without medication.

The Point: This is a tricky card for me; I've already confessed to a lifelong love of automobiles. That said, there are things you can do to save money even if—like me—you cannot force yourself to consider only the lowest cost per mile to get safely from point A to point B.

The Ideal: Decide on a couple of makes and models of cars you want. Tell the sales person you want an out-the-door price. Often they will give a price without sales tax, shipping charges, document preparation fees, etc. If they cannot understand out-the-door pricing, it's a sign you should go elsewhere. Remember, you are there to buy a car, not to make a new friend. After you get the out-the-door price, then discuss trade-in and financing. The odds are the dealer's financing will be more expensive and your trade-in worth less.

General rules to follow (check when considered):

____ Do you need to buy a new(er) car now? Huge amounts of money are wasted by this reasoning: I'm putting so much money into my old car, it is cheaper to get a new one (usually not!).

____ How important is saving money to you? The cheapest way to drive a fairly new car is to sell your old one privately and buy a one- to two-year-old car from a private party. But this is a hassle and carries certain risks.

____ Can a few inexpensive repairs or upgrades get you years longer from your current car: tires, a better sound system, a GPS system?

____ How many cars do you need? Are there alternatives in your area: car sharing, public transportation?

Be careful—if you decide to buy, follow these rules:

- Buy a reliable car (I like Consumer Reports for this information) no bigger than you need. Look at overall fuel mileage, not total miles you can drive on a full tank of gas (means only a big tank that weighs more and reduces mileage).
- Consider your tolerance for hassle versus saving money: Trading your old for a new car sold by a dealer and financing it there is the least hassle, but most expensive.
- Price down to the cheapest possible, not up to what the dealer says you can borrow. On financing: best = don't finance; better = shop for best financing; worst = finance through the dealer.
- Use all applicable NBI principles: clear pricing, no add-ons, no hidden charges, and get an "out-the-door" price. "Out-the-door-price" may confuse them—ask, "What don't you understand?"
- As a nod to NBI before you buy, ask what this destination charge thing is! Cars always have a destination charge—usually about $800. What other products get away with this crap? If you buy a refrigerator from Sears, are you charged $40 to ship it to the store? I once refused to buy a car until the dealer prepared new documents that clearly showed the destination charge in the price. Go for it.

NBI Guidance Focus CARD
CELL PHONES

ARNBism: If you can talk forever, how much is each minute worth?

The Point: Cell phones have taken over American society. There is no area where a replacement product—cell phone for landlines in this case—has so changed the pricing rules. Example: paying for an incoming call! I can't change cell phone dominance nor can I stop college students from running into me as they text while walking across the campus of Penn State. I can offer suggestions for managing the costs.

The Basic Decision: Does your current phone/plan get the job done? If so, don't get lured into newer bells and louder whistles. However, you may be able to negotiate a better deal. Try! Companies realize it is far easier and cheaper to keep a current customer than to find a new one. Get that rate reduced (you still can use some of the tips below if you must change).

Let's say you've carefully weighed the options and want a new plan/phone. Here are things you must do—check them off.

____ Decide on what features you really need and compare—this is not easy because figures often are confusing. Yes, virtually no companies kill the nines.

____ Demand a printout of how much your total monthly bill will be with normal assumptions, everything, not just, e.g., 500 minutes a month for a low monthly fee of $29.99. Exactly how much are all other costs, and what are they? Names can be very confusing.

____ What costs can they increase during your contract period?

____ Get, in writing, big print, how long your contract obligation is and how much it costs to leave early.

Additional questions to get a better deal and for the good of NBI:

- Why is my plan 300 minutes instead of five hours?
- Do I get charged for a call that does not go through?
- How many minutes do I get charged for a one-minute and three-second call?
- Do I get charged minutes checking messages? Even during the recorded prompt?
- Do you have rollover minutes—how do they work? Do they expire?
- What if I am traveling in a different time zone, in a different country?

NBI Guidance Focus CARD
AIRLINE TICKETS

ARNBism: Airline travel today is like a trip to the dentist, except they charge extra for fake Novocain.

The Point: I've been flying often for more than 30 years. The experience has become much less pleasant. There are two silver linings. In constant dollar terms, flying is cheaper and remains very safe. However, there are few areas more laden with bull. One example: a boldly advertised price that is the one-way price, but you must buy a roundtrip and pay other required costs. Typically the big print says $199, the fine print says $600 for the entire trip.

A Basic Decision: What is the principal goal for your trip? Are you willing to pay more to get a better routing or a more comfortable seat? This is an individual decision, but one that you should carefully assess.

After you follow the advice above, take these steps to maximize your chances of a successful flight.

____ Check multiple sources for the best price—airline websites, Expedia, etc. If possible, check often over a period of many weeks. Know what a good price is, so you can "grab" it when it becomes available. Give the nod to sites that make total prices absolutely clear. The airline I used most has a charge called "Taxes/Carrier-Imposed Fees."

____ Be sure you consider the total price for all passengers, including extra costs: checked bags, food purchased, better seats, taxes, etc.

____ What are the penalties for changes or cancellation? These can be huge. Often it will cost more to change a reservation than to forfeit the ticket.

___ Triple-check before you buy. You have to be quick and agile to get online deals. But you must be certain what you are buying. Many airline websites are cluttered and confusing. Sometimes I think I've found a great price, and it turns out I was missing a detail, such as a 7 p.m. departure and not the 7 a.m. departure I wanted.

___ Watch out for frequent flyer programs. Most are free to join and may provide some benefit. But do not spend a lot more money to accumulate points or miles. These can be a terrible deal. My principal program advertises free tickets for "as little as 22,500 miles." I never can find them for that—recently an international roundtrip cost 400,000 miles plus a $75 service fee!

___ Consider using the telephone. Many airlines now charge extra to buy a ticket over the phone. No one wants to waste money, but if you can get a better flight, cheaper for your family of five, this might be well worth it. Many telephone agents are great, others not. It takes effort to find the best deal. Politely say "no thank you," hang up and try again later if it seems like you're getting nowhere.

___ Take a deep breath: The flight probably will not be pleasant. It will be safe, and let's hope your destination makes it worthwhile.

NBI Guidance Focus CARD
MAGAZINE SUBSCRIPTIONS

ARNBism: Top secret: when does your subscription end?

The Point: It is a tough time for magazines, but Time, Vogue, People, welcome to the second decade of the 21st century! Magazines must adjust to this new information era like all the rest of us. Some will not make it. There are different information modes that are more convenient and do not kill trees.

Ask yourself the following about each magazine to which you subscribe—you may be able to drop some of them and/or switch to an e-version.

___ Do I read most of the magazine most of the time?

___ Can I get most of the content online, easier, with less clutter, and for less money?

___ I continue to subscribe mostly from inertia—because that's what I have always done?

___ Is there a lot of overlap among the magazines I receive? Drop the magazines that fail most of the above tests. Then assess remaining subscriptions according to the following NBI standards.

___ Does your subscription tell you clearly, in big print, exactly when your subscription expires?

___ Are there automatic renewals without telling you exact terms, including costs?

___ Are there solicitations for subscription extensions without telling you exact terms?

___ Are you solicited by fast talking "extend now or the world will end" salespeople?

Threaten to cancel if you have many checks above or with any renewal before six months or if price per issue and terms are not absolutely clear. Media companies have learned it's cheaper to keep existing customers than to find new ones.

NBI Guidance Focus CARD
VOTING

ARNBism: Listen between the lines.

The Point: Elections are important to the proper functioning of American society. NBI, when practiced by more people, aims to improve the information environment. Better information, in turn, should make elections more effective, ultimately creating the climate where government works better. There still will be disagreements and gridlock but not on the level the US has struggled with over the last several years. While the following guidelines will not always lead to a single choice—or to a political party preference—if you follow them, your choices should improve.

____ **Most things are gray, dammit:** Watch sweeping statements about actions candidates will take. For example, do they promise drastic changes immediately after taking office, changes they haven't the power to enact?

____ **Watch your political party legacy:** Chances are you adopted the political party of your parents. Take a hard look at whether this fits you at the present time.

____ **Filter the numbers and statistics:** Candidates often make deceptive, silly claims based on statistical information. Don't accept these. Politicians who have quick across-the-board solutions seldom have a workable plan.

____ **Rhetoric warning # 1—inspiration alone:** Leaders must inspire, but inspiration is not enough.

____ **Rhetoric warning # 2—the Trump tactic:** Donald Trump does this really effectively: State a virtually impossible premise, e.g., a healthy 20-year-old's aorta bursting. Then gain credibility by saying you doubt the aorta really burst, but then immediately switch to discussing the catastrophic consequences of all your blood being pumped where it does not belong.

___ **Balance local and national interests:** Elected officials do serve the folks back home, but they also must consider broader national interests, especially in our globalizing world.

___ **Admit they do not know:** Politics is complicated, and no one can know it all. Prudent "I don't know's" are a good sign.

___ **Balanced view of change:** Some change always is needed; be suspicious of those who call for too much or too little change.

___ **Be on the lookout for simple, quick solutions:** Democracies usually are slow and require approval at multiple levels.

___ **Balanced view of past successes:** Look at past successes, but don't ignore the failures. President Reagan helped create jobs but did not reduce the deficit. President Clinton helped produce economic growth but also sowed some of the seeds for a long housing market mess.

NBI Guidance Focus CARD
COLLEGE CHOICE/ADMISSION

ARNBism: NBI demands a better claim-to-fame than "student centered."

The Point: Full disclosure—because I am a college professor, I have a vested interest in having more smart students attend college. College is more expensive than ever and decisions about college more difficult. There is a movement—accelerating from the 1990s onward—for colleges to behave more like businesses, for example, college is like buying milk at a supermarket. I believe this is dangerous. I am certain this has increased NBI problems for colleges.

Basic Issue: $$$ and location. Can you afford to move away from home and attend full time? Often this is better, but it costs more and many cannot afford it. Balance status, cost, and value.

Important considerations (check when completed):

____ Think about the program, narrow it realistically: job prospects, ability, interests.

____ Find the percent of last year's graduates that found a job, and at what salaries.

____ Critically examine college data: surveys, success claims, faculty quality.

____ Get accurate information for number of applicants, acceptances, and attending.

____ Get accurate information about tuition costs (in and out of state) and living expenses.

____ Get accurate information about financial aid—how much and what kinds, and compared to total costs.

___ For ~18-year-olds—the ability of the student to handle this major transition must be considered.

___ Warning about for-profits—many charge much and deliver little; look into how competitive it is. If everyone is admitted, it's a red flag.

___ Get accurate information about who does the teaching—full-time professors, teaching assistants, level of education they have, etc.

___ What is the class size—get the mean and the median.

___ Watch "real-world experience" claims—they often misunderstand college.

___ "Student centered" is an overused slogan that usually is a poor substitute for explaining why a college is good.

Making the Final Choice

- Narrow it down to two or three choices—visit each again (unannounced).

- Observe a couple of classes on campus, talk to the students and faculty.

- Do detailed cost comparisons, including all financial aid offers.

- Don't be afraid to negotiate with good schools that accept you and get an "in-the-door price."

- Once you decide, don't stew about it; concentrate on doing well.

CHAPTER 10

CONCLUSIONS: BECOMING A WISER CITIZEN AND CONSUMER

This has not been a long book, and the last chapter will follow suit. Of course, this is due to Arnbi's tough love that demands brevity.

 Cramming a 162-page book into 360 pages is easy to do, but it wastes time, trees, and diminishes understanding.

Heeding this warning is not easy—college professors tend to be long-winded. There could be an online NBI encyclopedia with Arnbi's thumb pointing upwards on the spine of each of 12 volumes.

The volumes as they appeared on your iPad would be bound in beautiful Corinthian leather. Certainly there is more than enough material and piles of bull to level before we sleep. As you have seen, NBI is most effective as a mass-participatory activity. I've introduced the fundamental ideas so you and thousands of others can demand better information. If we make these NBI demands on car dealers, politicians, supermarkets, and so forth, we can change their behavior. Buyers will avoid that $199 a month car lease because it violates NBI rules, such as:

- using nines—make it $200
- not revealing how long the lease is
- a $4,999 "origination" charge is required at the beginning of the lease
- you may drive only 7,500 miles a year or pay a surcharge
- the rate includes a cash incentive available only to college students
- many other conditions are not legible (or audible)

Over the last quarter century, I have supervised 30 undergraduate honors theses, some longer than this book. One of the most frequent warnings I offer to these students is that their concluding sections tend to run out of gas, saying almost nothing except for a brief repetition of a few points made earlier. A final chapter should do more than repeat but still remain brief.

Almost everyone who writes a book wants brisk sales. I am no exception. However, I get very angry when I see authors, sports stars, or entertainment celebrities pitching products they know little about and probably do not believe in. I might express a personal preference for products and services based on my own experiences but will always remember I am a sample of one and a skewed sample at that. And I will use NBI principles.

Applying NBI rules is not always easy. I want to highlight four problem areas, likely roadblocks along the route to NBI.

1. Humor—part of a combination punch?

There may be a need for an entire book on this subject. Many advertisements, even some political campaign ads, use humor as a low-key way to get your attention. That may be fine as long as you still use NBI principles to assess information after you've begun to pay attention.

A widely broadcast television commercial for Capital One credit cards features pitch person and actor Alec Baldwin. In one of these commercials, he promises a young lady that her flight "comes with a private island," but when she asks, "Really?" he responds, "No, it comes with a hat." The commercials are very funny; I confess I look forward to seeing them in part because I am a fan of Mr. Baldwin. However, a humorous introduction must not blind us to subsequent claims made in the ad. Two claims stand out in these Capital One commercials:

- We do not have blackout dates; use our points on any flight, any airline, anytime. Sounds great, especially since you get double points for certain purchases! You earn two points for each dollar you spend, and each point is worth one cent.[77] The real question is how many points it takes for that hard-to-get airplane seat. The results can be huge; you'd have to charge $50,000 to get a $1,000 plane ticket for "free!"
- These ads have a lot of fine print that flashes across the TV screen so quickly that it offers far too little opportunity to assess it.

---

77 http://thepointsguy.com/2011/10/capital-one-venture-card-review/

2. Prejudices and small sample sizes obstruct NBI

An important element of analytical thinking, sampling, and many other aspects of NBI is the idea that people must move beyond their own individual situations and experiences. This can be difficult. History is replete with villains, even some extremely smart people, who were unable to do this; an example is Hitler and his pathological hatred of Jews. NBI requires making this leap: understanding that your experiences usually are not typical. Such feelings—prejudices—do not have to be negative. Consider a Chinese-American high school student who is a whiz at math and can't dribble a basketball to save his life. This student's best friend should guard against generalizing even when it comes to positive impressions of a best friend. In this case, was there a pre-conceived notion that Asians are great in science classes, but poor in athletic ability. Self-fulfilling prophecies are part of the human need for simplicity.

3. NBI does not mean maximum information

NBI does not mean maximum information. Maybe I should have called this book "optimal information." Information is more complex than ever in the 21st century. And we need a greater ability to understand, to parse things. We must think analytically and demand standards so we can see our options and accurately assess that widget we wish to buy. But we also should be careful not to go too far.

A couple of years ago I was watching a report on CNN morning news about a large group of distinguished scientists who had evaluated new evidence that a giant meteorite hit the earth tens of millions of years ago causing the extinction of the dinosaurs. The scientists concluded that the evidence was overwhelming. The CNN reporter went on to present the "other side" to this story. To use a legal concept, the preponderance of evidence was on the scientists' side. All sides are not equal! The positive goal of being fair coupled with love of sensationalism can create the misperception that all positions are equally valid and deserve equal time.

4. Balancing change against inaction

NBI, if used by enough of us, can produce a number of benefits. One of the most important is balancing inaction against too rapid change. This requires a more enlightened citizenry that votes more intelligently.

Here's a simple example based on something we're all familiar with—gasoline prices. The US. federal government introduced a gasoline tax in 1932, and we've had one ever since.

Year	Price per gal.	Fed. Tax per gal.	% of tax
1932	10¢	1¢	10%
2014	$3.80	18.4¢	4.8%

The impact of the tax on the average driver *decreased* dramatically, from 10% to less than 5%. Should the rate have been a constant 10%? The U.S. has thousands of laws that remain on the books even though they are stunningly outdated.

The other extreme can be seen when Congress and the president agree on a new law and pass it in October of a presidential election year. It might be a good law that addresses serious problems. Then in November we have another election. In February of the following year, a new Congress and new president agree on major changes to the law. Of course, they have the legal right to do this.

What's wrong with making such a change so quickly? Business will ask: How can we plan investment when the rules keep changing? Those who passed the first law will say there was far too little time to see if the old law would work. This can be like stopping a 14-day prescription after three days because there's been no improvement in the patient's health.

We must achieve a far better balance between retaining outmoded laws decades beyond their useful life and changing laws at the drop of a hat. NBI can help with this balance. Most decisions should be made somewhere in the middle, a gray area of compromise. We don't want government to regulate every comma on every food label. Instead, we must vote with our shopping dollars, buying products with good, clear nutrition labels. Government should prohibit teaser mortgages that start out at $499 per month and balloon to $1,000 after four years, but home buyers also should read the fine print, demand an explanation, and realize there is no free money.

Finishing Up

Recently, after demanding and receiving an NBI-acceptable price, I bought SiriusXM Satellite Radio for my car. Sirius provides a large selection of stations and near-perfect sound quality, but the commercials! Some are alright, but many are just ridiculous and violate almost every NBI rule: British accents, unspecified shipping charges, disclaimers that sound like a recording played at triple speed, and so forth.

This *composite hypothetical* gives you the idea. It begins, "Guys, certainly you want a full head of hair." Then it quotes from a "leading dermatologist" who says, "squeeze this amazing all-natural purple cream on your scalp as you drive home, and I guarantee you'll see longer hair within two hours." And then the claims become even more absurd! Effective regulation in this case probably would be impossible, but if enough people use NBI, these silly sales pitches will be ignored and provide nothing more than a good laugh.

Along with my humor, sarcasm, and exasperation, I hope you have seen that, underneath it all, I am at least an optimist and probably an idealist. That's what inspired me to become a college professor and to try to understand and explain things. But there remain massive piles of bull to attack. Arnbi provides a number of techniques. And I hope in your mind's eye you can see Arnbi advising you.

 Applying NBI principles will not be easy. It is a long-term effort. Sometimes it seems as if the odds are against success. In talking with dozens of people, including many students, the most frequent reaction dealt with my discussion of the power and danger of acronyms. Many people said something like, "That's so true—I never thought of it." Therefore, with Arnbi's permission and guidance, I have written a poem about acronyms. I venture into poetry in part to try to win over my colleagues in the arts and humanities, many of whom have no use for numbers; they believe if you can count it, it's not worth thinking about. One part of me wishes this were true, but my rational side wins the argument. In the 21st century our choice will not be between using and avoiding numbers. Instead, the best we can hope for is numbers that are reasonably accurate, correctly interpreted, and put into context.

 In the modern world, numbers will be used. The best feasible outcome is better use of them.

I have always liked poetry. I wonder whether there is a name for someone who likes poetry and statistics. I'll let my critics supply the correct descriptor.

Acronyms undefined,
amplified through rhyme,
repeated over time,

peddled online,
bring cognitive decline.

Here's another NBI-related poem contributed by Casey Graml,[78] a recent graduate of Penn State and former student of mine:

Arnbi uncovered the hedge of hope,
and sought to share it with the world.
With so much bull it was hard to cope,
until the NBI flag was unfurled.
He traveled the world through sleet and rain,
to bring more accurate information.
From bull-laden info you must abstain,
so spread the word without hesitation.

Finally, my friends, let me be quite frank. No-Bull Information is an exponentially difficult concept to have shared with you. It has required 110% of your attention. My experience with a student just yesterday proves the value of NBI. She was able to achieve up to a stunning 57% decline in her use of BLI expressions in her speech.

STOP!

TAKE A DEEP BREATH,

Then go to the next page.

---

78 Casey's help was invaluable. The second poem was written by him. Any shortcomings are attributable to my "tinkering."

While reading the previous paragraph, you should have wondered what is going on! Has this professor finally lost his mind? The paragraph violates about as many NBI rules as you can fit in the space provided. Look at the red below.

My friends, let me be quite frank.

No-Bull Information is an exponentially difficult concept to have shared with you. It has required 110% of your attention. My experience with a student just yesterday proves the value of NBI. She was able to achieve up to a stunning 57% decline in her use of BLI expressions in her speech.[79]

No-Bull Information is a way of coping more effectively with the flood of information that defines our new, chaotic, information-dense environment. NBI will not lead to the same answers for everyone. It does not favor any particular political or economic persuasion. NBI can help each individual to understand what is best for her/him.[80] What works for you as one person must consider seven billion other people on planet earth, each trying to find their route through the information labyrinth. Ultimately, the success of this book depends upon NBI's effectiveness as a tool for handling the most serious abuses of phrase and fact.

---

79 See NBI Guidance Card on "Word Warnings."
80 I am still alphabetizing pronouns.

Piles of Bull but Arnbi is ready

John Gamble, Ph.D.
Distinguished Professor of Political Science and International Law
The Behrend College
Penn State University
Erie, PA 16563

CPSIA information can be obtained at www.ICGtesting.com
Printed in the USA
LVOW06*2241010115

421105LV00008B/26/P